Understar  *y*

The unchangeable truth about marriage and sexuality is in our days under a general attack by the enemies of God and His Revelation. Since that time, the Church has defended this Divine truth through apologetics. In our days, there is an urgent need of apologetics in defense of the truth especially about marriage and sexuality. Marriage and family, being the vital cell of human society and of the Holy Church, are attacked largely because their natural and obvious meaning is distorted by modern ideological totalitarianism. *Understanding Marriage and Family: A Catholic Perspective* by Fr. Sebastian Walshe, O.Praem., is a true Catholic apologia for marriage and family, showing in a convincing and dialogical manner the beauty of their meaningfulness as planned and created by the infinite wisdom of God the Creator and the Redeemer. This book will surely be of great benefit to everyone who wants sincerely to know the true and unchanging meaning of marriage and family, so that moral beauty and moral health might be restored to the entire family of humankind of our day.

✠ ATHANASIUS SCHNEIDER, Auxiliary Bishop of the Archdiocese of St. Mary in Astana

Ascending upon both reason and faith, Fr. Sebastian Walshe, O.Praem., with providential clarity, charity, and certainty, dismantles the desolation of lives unmoored from human nature, and marriages divorced from their divine inspiration, proposing anew to all willing to hear, the freeing and fulfilling proposal of Christian marriage in all its solidity and sublimity. Look within to regain hope, recover communion, and rediscover the fullness of married joy!

✠ THOMAS J. PAPROCKI, Bishop of the Diocese of Springfield, IL

In the midst of so much confusion and darkness about marriage and family among Catholics and non-Catholics alike, this book by Fr. Walshe brings much appreciated clarity and light. His precise definitions, cogent explanations and convincing answers to the key objections make this book an indispensable handbook for parents, educators and all those who are seeking to re-propose to the world the truth, beauty and goodness about marriage and family.

✠ JAMES S. WALL, Bishop of the Diocese of Gallup, NM

Finally, a book that provides clear definitions, makes incisive distinctions, and anticipates all the main objections hurled at both marriage and the family. This is a complete field manual that brings Father Walshe's characteristic warm style and cool logic to the most important battle in the culture war. If you want to defend what St. John Paul II called "the first and the most important path that man walks," look no farther. Highly recommended.

— PATRICK COFFIN, Host, and co-founder of CoffinNation.com

Understanding Marriage & Family

Understanding Marriage & Family

A Catholic Perspective

SEBASTIAN WALSHE, O.PRAEM.

AROUCA
PRESS

ISBN: 978-1-7770523-6-2 (pbk)
ISBN: 978-1-7770523-7-9 (hardcover)

Arouca Press
PO Box 55003
Bridgeport PO
Waterloo, ON N2J3G0
Canada
www.aroucapress.com

Send inquiries to info@aroucapress.com

Cover and book design by Michael Schrauzer
Cover image: Bartolomé Esteban Perez Murillo,
"The Holy Family with a Bird," detail, ca. 1650
(modified from Wikimedia Commons).

TABLE OF CONTENTS

ACKNOWLEDGEMENTS

FIRST, I WANT TO THANK ABBOT EUGENE HAYES,
O. Praem., and my Prior, Fr. Chrysostom Baer, O. Praem., for encouraging me and allowing me to publish this book. I am also indebted
to Fr. Victor Szczurek, O. Praem., for carefully reading over the manuscript, and to Fr. John Henry Hanson, O. Praem., for his frequent
words of encouragement and advice during the publishing process.
In a special way I owe thanks to Dr. Michael Augros who has been
a friend and intellectual mentor for many years. I learned or refined
many of the concepts and arguments found in the opening chapters through my discussions and correspondence with him. Finally,
I want to thank all of my students from my marriage and family
course throughout the years. They have pushed and challenged me
on many points during the course, and many of the objections and
answers found in this book are the fruit of those classroom discussions. I could not have written this book without them. May God
reward all of you for your contributions!

INTRODUCTION

THIS BOOK IS ABOUT THE FAMILY. FIRST, A word should be said about what I mean by family in this book. By the term "family" I mean, first of all, the communion of a husband, his wife, and their children. The word "family" has many usages and meanings in modern language, and I will consider some of these at the appropriate place. But the definition of family I have given is the first definition of family: it is the meaning of family to which all other definitions of family must ultimately refer.

Many people today have difficulty understanding the meaning, purpose or worth of the family as I have defined it. Some people consider this definition of family to be the source of injustice towards persons: both persons within and outside of this family. For example, some think that it is a fundamentally male dominated model of human life that is unjust to the women within the family. Again, some think that it fails to take into consideration the experiences of those who fall outside of the statistical norms of human life, and so ends up marginalizing them just because they are different from most people. Some people think of the family as I have defined it as something harmful to human flourishing: it is limiting and prevents the whole range of human possibilities of love and relationships. Some people just think that the family as I have defined it is outdated and is no longer useful or relevant to modern life. If you are among those who, for whatever reason, think the definition of family I have given should be discarded, I encourage you to keep reading with an open mind. Perhaps there are some important things you may not have considered that will come along as you continue reading. On the other hand, if you are someone who thinks the definition of family I have given should be defended, then I ask you too to continue reading with an open mind: try to understand, as I hope I have done, the legitimate and serious difficulties of others who disagree with you. And if you know someone who thinks differently about the family, then I hope that this book will help you to clarify your own thoughts and communicate them more perfectly.

In sum, the purpose of this book is to help modern people understand once more the meaning of the family as well as its beauty and worth. I will use two different, but complementary paths to accomplish this goal.

First, this book will consider the human family in light of truths that can be known, in principle, by anyone of any culture or place or belief system. These are the truths discoverable by the light of human reason. They do not come from the Bible or assent to any particular religion. For example, the truth that a man and a woman are naturally capable of begetting children together, the truth that fathers and mothers ought to protect and provide for their children, and to do this together, and so on, are truths that can be known without some special act of faith or formation in some particular culture.

The second path I will take is the path accessible to those who accept divine revelation, especially as it is found in the Bible. For those who do not accept Christian revelation, this part will largely be hypothetical, yet it may still be instructive for someone who wants to understand the Christian perspective more fully. To follow this path requires faith in what is revealed in the Bible about the family. For example, the truth that the relationship between a husband and his wife are a sign of the relationship between Christ and the Church, or the truth that the relationship between a father and his son is a sign of the relationship between the first two Persons of the Trinity are truths that can be known only through an act of faith.

What is the relationship between these two paths and why am I using both? In this book, I will treat these paths as sequentially related: the second path coming after the first path. I have three main reasons for following this method: first, because revelation presupposes and builds upon what can be known by reason. Every word in the Bible has its meaning derived from something first known in the natural world by human reason. Jesus himself seems to acknowledge this when he explains supernatural realities in terms of natural ones, like mustard seeds and trees, etc. Clearly, I cannot understand the relationship between the Father and the Son in the Trinity if I have no idea what the words "father" and "son" mean. And we first learn the meanings of these words from the natural world around us, not from revelation.

The second reason why I am following this method is because the truths of revelation (if they are truly revealed by God) complete and perfect the truths knowable by reason. God is the author of both the natural world and of authentic revelation, and so both ways of coming to know the family should harmonize. Thus, this book seeks to explain God's plan for the human family from revelation in a way which completes and explains more fully the things we can already know about the family from a natural perspective. God has a plan for everything he has made. Human beings can discover part of that plan by considering natural, created things and the relationships among them. But a merely natural or human perspective on creation must necessarily be incomplete and partial, since it cannot discover the hidden intentions in the mind of God. Revelation gives us God's own perspective of the plan he has for the things he has made. For God has revealed things not only about himself, but also about creatures and how they relate to him. Theology gives a more complete and comprehensive account of the plan which God has for the things he has made. A Theology of the family will therefore give a more complete and comprehensive account of God's plan for the human family.[1]

The third main reason why I begin by following the path accessible to reason alone is because this book is not directed exclusively to those who believe in Christian revelation. It is also directed to anyone with good will and an open mind who wants to understand the nature, purpose and worth of the family. By including a distinct part of this book which does not presuppose faith in any particular religion or culture, readers from any background can find many helpful and useful explanations which serve to clarify and deepen

---

1   "Willed by God in the very act of creation, marriage and the family are interiorly ordained to fulfillment in Christ." *Familiaris Consortio 3.*

their understanding of the meaning of the family. Such a method allows for "common ground" among believers and unbelievers alike. And this is already a very good start.

So all three of these reasons help to explain why it is useful to first look at the family from the perspective of human reason and then from the perspective of divine revelation.

Because many of the arguments, explanations and observations I will make in this book naturally will raise several questions and difficulties, I will attempt to anticipate the most common or significant of these throughout the book. To accomplish this, I will raise difficulties and questions at the end or even in the middle of some chapters and try to provide clear and understandable solutions to them.

CUSTOMARY WAYS OF THINKING

Before I go on, a word should be said about the customary ways of thinking people can adopt from their environment. It is obvious that the way people speak and think around you can affect how you think and speak. We have a natural tendency to want to agree with those around us, especially those who are prominent. As a result of this tendency, we often acquire habits of thinking which are not founded in our experience of things, but rather are the result of our desire to accept what people say, and to be pleasing and acceptable to those around us. Aristotle described this influence of customs on our thinking in this way:

> Now things heard take effect in accord with custom. For as we are accustomed, so we demand things to be said. And what are against these customs seem to be not agreeable, but unintelligible and rather foreign because of a lack of experience of them. For the customary seems better known to us. And how great is the force which custom has, the laws show, in which mythical and childish things are more forceful than knowledge about them, because of custom. Now some will not accept speakers if one does not speak mathematically. Others if one

does not speak by way of examples. And some demand a
poet be introduced as a witness. And some demand that
all things be said exactly, whereas to others exactness
is annoying, either because they are not able to make
connections or because of pettiness.[2]

This customary way of thinking is sometimes called "intellectual custom." Intellectual custom can be defined as a quasi-natural
habit of the mind, dependent upon the customs in which someone
exists, which inclines them to accept some assertion as known or
better-known. When someone is speaking under the influence of
custom they say things like: "I don't like those views, they offend
me" or "those ideas seem strange to me." So it is very important if
we are to get at the truth that we look honestly at the ways in which
the views of those around us can affect our own judgments.

As regards matters pertaining to family and marriage, it is obvious to everyone that the ways of thinking have radically changed
over the past few decades. Take, for example, the following two
propositions: 1) sexual intercourse for the sake of pleasure alone is
good; and 2) persons of the same sex can marry. Popular opinion
about the truth or falsity of these two propositions has changed
radically in the past few decades. Yet one thing that we can all
agree on is that right now the major means of social communication in western nations treat both these propositions as true and
certain, if not self-evident. In contrast, there has been practical
unanimity throughout human history over diverse nations and
cultures that sexual intercourse is for the sake of procreation, and
that marriage can only exist between a man and woman. G.K.
Chesterton used to say that the traditional views of our ancestors
was merely a form of democracy for the dead. In a democratic
nation no one is excluded from voting on account of accident of
birth: tradition simply adds that someone's vote ought not to be
excluded on account of accident of death. The views about marriage in modern western nations stand as an historical anomaly

2 Metaphysics II.3.

when set up against the practical unanimity of the nations, cultures and religions throughout recorded human history, to say nothing of the modern non-western cultures. Whenever two large groups of people have such strikingly opposed views, it is obvious that intellectual custom has had a strong influence on the thinking of one or both groups. Therefore, it is especially important to approach this topic with an open mind and honestly to acknowledge how the views of those around you have affected your own positions. Only when each person is willing to do this can the truth be sought honestly and sincerely.

So that's enough by way of introduction. Let's begin.

PART I
The Path of Reason

1

Understanding and Clarifying the Words We Are Using

ONE OF THE GREATEST SOURCES OF CONFUSION and error in discussion is something Aristotle referred to as the fallacy of equivocation: that is, the mistake of confusing two distinct things because they have the same name. Here is a simple example to make my point. Everyone has a right to be happy. But heroin makes people happy. Therefore, people have a right to take heroin. In this argument (called a syllogism), the word "happy" has two different meanings. In the first statement "happy" means that which ultimately perfects human nature. In the second statement "happy" means a particular kind of emotional or physical pleasure. Because not every emotional or physical pleasure actually perfects human nature, the argument does not follow. And the source of confusion was the fact that two distinct concepts were signified using the same name. Something similar can happen in discussions about the family, and so if we are to avoid unnecessary confusion and mistakes, it is important first of all to explain the different but related meanings of the word "family."

But before we do that, I want to head off an initial problem. As I am setting down and explaining the definitions of family and marriage, many possible objections might be raised against one or another part of these definitions. For example, someone might object to the assertion that marriage is for the sake of begetting children because infertile couples can marry. I promise, I will try to anticipate and consider the most significant objections to the definitions I am about to set down. However, if I tried to do that while explaining the definitions, there would be so many tangents that it would cloud the basic explanation I am providing, and it would impede your ability simply to see the reality I am trying to signify. In some sense, definitions are simply letting you know what I mean by a certain word, and also the way I think it has been used by people who speak the same language. Even if you don't agree that I have given the right definition, at least you will know what I mean by these words in this book, and that is already helpful. So, if you like, take these definitions as merely provisional. The main purpose of this section is not to prove that these are the only proper definitions of marriage and family, but rather to make clear the distinctions between various definitions of marriage and family so that there will be less likelihood of confusion when I discuss these things. At the end of the chapter, there will be a section for considering objections, and I hope the responses to these objections will be sufficient to manifest that the definitions I have given here correspond to something in reality, and are not merely verbal fabrications.

THE FIRST MEANING OF FAMILY

The first meaning of family, the one I will use as the basic meaning of family throughout this book, is *a communion of a husband, his wife, and their children*. Each part of this definition could use some explanation.

A *communion* is a multitude of persons in which each person somehow lives or shares the life of every other person. A communion is more intimate than a mere community. In a mere community, there is a common goal, something which unites the persons, but there is no true sharing of life. So a communion is a community plus the sharing of life. For example, family members live together, and know about each other's lives and love each other. Later on I will consider in greater depth this concept of communion, but here, it suffices to say that communion means more than just people acting in unison toward some common goal.

The words *a husband and his wife* are in the definition of family, instead of say "father and mother" to indicate that marriage is part of the definition of family. It is true that couples who cohabitate and have children resemble a family, but the very fact that they have not promised to remain together in a stable union shows that they are not a family in the full sense of the word. They just happen to be together now because they don't have a better option. Where stability is lacking, unity is lacking. And where unity is lacking there is no *communion*: how could someone truly share a life with another person who might just get up and leave? Therefore, in order to have the full notion of family, there must be stability. And that means that the couple must have made some kind of outward and exclusive commitment to remain together. In other words, they must be in a marriage. Of course, marriage here does not just mean a legal document or a ceremony: it refers to the moral intention to remain together in a stable union (though some kind of public or outward manifestation of their exclusive union seems necessary so that their children and others in the community can see that they are married). The fact that to the degree that persons have less unity and stability among them, to the same degree do they cease to have the notion of a family shows that unity and stability is part of the very meaning of "family." This unity and stability comes out in the expression *a husband and his wife*.

Why does the definition of *family* include *their children*? Because a husband and wife are more properly called a "couple" than a family before they have children. True, we will speak sometimes about a married couple as being a family, but ordinarily it is only when children come along that we refer to "so and so's family." And couples often say when they are trying to have kids that they want to "start a family." So "family" in the full sense includes children. *Their children* first of all refers to their biological children, but also includes children by adoption, since children who are adopted and permanent members of the family enter into the communion between the parents.[1]

---

1   It is true, however, that the first idea we have of someone's children are their biological children. This is not to assert that adopted children are loved less then natural children, but it is to recognize the primacy of natural begetting. A sign of this is that couples who adopt children affirm that they love their adopted children "as if they were their own" or "as much as their natural children." They never say about their natural children that they love them "as if they were adopted."

RELATED MEANINGS OF FAMILY

But what about grandparents and aunts and uncles and cousins? Aren't they also part of what we mean by someone's "family"? Yes, but this would be a different meaning of family, more what we would typically call an "extended family." Sometimes, when speaking to our own cousins or relatives, we will refer to "our family" as opposed to "their family," meaning our immediate family as distinct from their immediate family or our extended family. So "family" clearly has two different but related meanings here: the first meaning is one's immediate family (defined above) the second meaning is one's extended family, which includes grandparents, aunts, uncles and cousins. Nevertheless, this second meaning of family depends upon the first. The only reason we call these more distant relatives "family" is because of their relationship to our immediate family members. Our grandparents are our family because they are our parent's parents. Our aunts and uncles are our family because they are our parent's siblings. Our cousins are our family because they are the children of our parent's siblings.

How about close friends. Don't we sometimes call them family? Yes, not as commonly, but here again we have an example of a different but related meaning. When we call friends our "family" we are using the term "family" more as a metaphor, that is, a word which is carried over from one thing to another because of some likeness between them. So friends are not family in the proper sense of the word. In this case, because we notice that the love we have for our close friends is like the love we have (or at least should have) for our family members, and because we often live with our friends in a way like we live with family members, we transfer the word "family" over from our blood family to our friendships. So here again, the reason why we use the word "family" at all to designate certain friends is because of a likeness to "family" as defined above. The communion of a husband, his wife, and their children is always the reference point for every other significant use of the word "family." Notice also this difference: while we might call a friend our "brother," "sister," or even "father" or "mother," we would never call our friends "husband" or "wife" (except perhaps jokingly). There is something unique about marriage, the primary relationship which is the foundation of all true families. And so there is an aspect of family life, namely marriage, which cannot be simply identified with friendship.

THE MEANING OF MARRIAGE

Since the definition of family presupposes an understanding of husband and wife, and since a husband and wife are understood in terms of marriage (a husband is a married man, while a wife is a married woman), it follows that we must define marriage in order to more perfectly understand the meaning of family. Marriage is the *lifelong communion of a man and woman, established by their free consent, for the sake of the generation and education of children.* Here I am defining marriage as something knowable by human reason unaided by faith.[2] Later on I will define the sacrament of marriage, which is based upon this natural understanding of marriage, but includes reference to a supernatural institution and purpose. But as I said at the beginning of the book, I am going to follow the path accessible to human reason before considering what God has revealed about marriage and the family.

As with the definition of family, each part of this definition could use some clarification. First of all, marriage is *for the sake of the generation and education of children.* Modern people often have a hard time with this part of the definition of marriage, mostly because of cultural influences. As I mentioned above, to consider the difficulties surrounding this part of the definition here would be a significant tangent, so for the sake of maintaining the flow of the explanation of the definition of marriage, I will consider a number of these difficulties at the end of this chapter. Here I simply want to point out that loving one another, living together, even raising children together do not make someone married. Two friends could promise to love one another, and even live together for a lifetime and that wouldn't make them married. A brother and sister could promise to raise the children of their deceased sibling together, yet that wouldn't

---

2   A sign of this is that many diverse faiths, and those with no faith at all, have acknowledged marriage as defined here.

make them married. Marriage has reference to the act of begetting children. When two people promise the exclusive right over one another's bodies for the acts that are apt to generate children, then they are married. All those other aspects: loving one another, living together for a lifetime, raising children together, follow from this fundamental commitment that is for the sake of begetting children. The *education of children* is the proper common activity of spouses. And the central common activity of any healthy marriage will be the activity of educating children. This education is primarily moral, so it has as its goal leading the children to human perfection.

I have already mentioned that family is a communion. Here we see that the source of the communion in a family is the communion of the husband and wife. But why does marriage have to be *lifelong*? Many people get married and subsequently get divorced, yet we don't say that they were never really married before the divorce. Here the descriptive term *lifelong* means that the spouses must **intend** to remain united for their entire lives at the time they marry. If this is lacking, then the union would not be a marriage properly speaking (though perhaps someone might call it a "marriage" in a diminished sense of the term, but not the full and proper sense which is being defined here). We can also see from another part of the definition of marriage why it has to be lifelong. For if marriage is *for the sake of the education of children*, it is clear that this is substantially a lifelong common activity. Even parents of grown children continue to educate their grown children by providing an example of how to live virtuously in the next stage of their lives (for example, how to handle retirement, how to be good grandparents, or how to endure the hardships of old age and death). Finally, because marriage is a kind of *communion*, it must also be lifelong. For communion implies oneness of life, and nobody wants to live only part of their own life. So too, one who shares the life of another in communion wants to share the whole of their life. Without this, it would not be a true communion. So from all three of these considerations, we can see that marriage demands a lifelong communion. And this is not because of some extrinsic imposition by the mere will of those who enter into marriage: it is demanded by what marriage is in itself; it is intrinsic to the nature of marriage. From this it follows that marriage is indissoluble.

Because marriage is *for the sake of generating children*, this *lifelong communion* is obviously between a *man and a woman*. This part of the definition of marriage, which has been considered self-evident over most of human history, has remained all but unchallenged until modern times. The reason for the denial of this part of the definition of marriage in recent times is found in the denial that marriage is for the sake of begetting children. We will treat these issues at the end of this chapter.

Finally, the *communion* must be *established by their free consent* for there to be a marriage. Marriage is not merely the consequence of blind forces, instincts and inclinations, but a consequence of the fact that human beings have reason and can understand the purposes of their actions. One consequence of begetting children is the duty to raise them. And, as we have already seen, this requires a lifetime commitment. Such a commitment could not be entered into without free and full consent.

One thing that comes out clearly after considering the parts of the definition of marriage is the fact that the definition holds together by itself, and seems to be founded in the very nature of things. All of the elements of the definition of marriage go back to the fact that it is for the sake of the generation of children. This is what unifies the entire definition and gives a reasonable basis for holding the other parts together. It is obvious that human beings (and all living things) have a natural inclination to reproduce. Without this inner inclination, our species, and all species, would go extinct. Moreover, human children, unlike the offspring of many other animals require two parents for their well-being. Even in a one-parent household, that parent must enlist the help of someone else either to provide for the children, or to watch and care for them as they provide for them. In other words, they have to find a "substitute spouse." So the definition of marriage is not some artificial construct like the definition of a car or some man-made artifact. Artificial things like cars are man-made both insofar as this particular car is man-made, and insofar as the very "what it is to be car" is a product of human reason. Marriage is man-made in the sense that this particular marriage is entered into by the free consent of the spouses, but the very "what it is to be marriage" is not man made, but discovered in human nature itself. In fact, the very word "nature" is derived from the word meaning "birth." Nothing could be more natural than begetting children in the way they should be begotten for their flourishing, namely within a family. This is why marriages and families have existed from the beginning of human nature: before any states or countries were formed, there were men and women living together for the sake of begetting and raising their own children. Some politician did not make up marriage: human persons at all times and places have found themselves naturally inclined to marry.

RECENT NEW USES OF THE WORDS MARRIAGE AND FAMILY

Only recently other usages of the words "marriage" and "family" have been introduced into modern vocabulary. These usages have not been introduced because of the natural development of human language, but rather as the result of an intentional effort by those in power to alter vocabulary. And so these new meanings of the words "marriage" and "family" have been mostly the result of political efforts and media-driven, social-engineering programs. Through this change in vocabulary, the intention is to alter patterns of thinking about marriage and the family. The insightful dialogue between Humpty Dumpty and Alice in Lewis Carroll's "Through the Looking Glass" is apropos here:

> "There's glory for you!" said Humpty Dumpty.
> "I don't know what you mean by 'glory,'" Alice said.
> Humpty Dumpty smiled contemptuously. "Of course you don't—till I tell you. I meant 'there's a nice knock-down argument for you!'"
> "But 'glory' doesn't mean 'a nice knock-down argument,'" Alice objected.

"When **I** use a word," Humpty Dumpty said, in rather a scornful tone, "it means just what I choose it to mean — neither more nor less."

"The question is," said Alice, "whether you **can** make words mean so many different things."

"The question is," said Humpty Dumpty, "which is to be master — that's all."[3]

Words have power over minds, the power to be "master," because of the potential for equivocation. By using the same word for different realities, the likelihood of thinking that they are the same reality is significantly increased. This is especially true when the persons using the words are not used to carefully defining their words. Take this simple example. The word "discrimination" used to be a positive term used to describe the act of carefully noticing significant differences between things, and treating different things according to their significant differences. For example, a grocer might discriminate between healthy and unhealthy produce. Understood in this sense, discrimination is an act of the virtue of prudence. But at some point the word ceased being used that way (especially in the major means of social communication), and was used almost exclusively to refer to the act of noticing insignificant differences and unjustly treating persons as unequal based upon those differences. Thus, discrimination became a negative term to describe racism, sexism, etc. Understood in this latter sense, discrimination is an act of the vice of injustice. Therefore, people today often confuse the two meanings and when someone is discriminating in the first sense, they accuse them of doing something unjust.

NEW USES OF THE WORD "MARRIAGE"

What are some of the new uses of the words "marriage" and "family"? Many recent uses of the term "marriage" are supposed to include two persons of the same sex (two men or two women), or even more than two persons. Usually it is supposed that these

---

3   Lewis Carroll, *Through the Looking Glass*, chapter 6.

persons have some romantic interest in one another. Their union is not for the sake of begetting children (though raising children is often considered a right for those in such unions). Rather, the motive of these unions is mutual love, satisfaction or enrichment. This union need not be intended as lifelong to constitute a "marriage" though in some cases this is what people do intend. Finally, such a union is not rooted in the natural inclination to beget and raise children. Thus, "marriage" in this sense is essentially something artificial, in which the very "what it is to be marriage" is established either by the state or by the will of the individual persons who contract this union.

Putting these elements together we can assemble the following new definition: "marriage" is the union of two or more persons for the sake of romantic love and mutual enrichment, the nature of this union being defined, established and recognized by legal contract or by mutual agreement and free consent of the persons.[4] There are some likenesses between this definition and the original definition of marriage given above, but there are also some extremely important differences. And based upon these important differences one ought to discriminate (in the positive sense of the term) between them. One likeness is that both definitions are about a union between persons. Another likeness is the fact that sexual desire (presumably including the intention to employ one's reproductive organs together) is part of the intention of these persons. A third likeness is the fact that this union is entered into by the free consent of the persons. A fourth likeness is the desirability of this union being recognized and protected by law.

But now let's consider some differences. A first important difference is that the purpose of marriage in the original sense is procreation (and education) of children. The purpose of "marriage" in this new sense is romantic love and mutual enrichment. A second

---

4   One might also provide alternative definitions. For example, one might wish to restrict "marriage" to two persons; or one might wish to indicate that romantic love is not essential. However, for the most part this definition seems to correspond to the chief new sense of "marriage" as advanced by government agencies and used today by major media.

important difference is that marriage in the original sense is between a man and a woman, while "marriage" in this new sense is between persons regardless of gender. A third important difference is that marriage in the original sense is natural, and arises spontaneously from the very nature of our species to procreate and raise one's own children. But "marriage" in the new sense is the result merely of human choice, and so takes the form of a kind of legal contract created by the state rather than a moral union rooted in human nature which is merely recognized by the state. A fourth important difference is that marriage in the original sense is lifelong by its nature, while "marriage" in this new sense is not.

So when we put these definitions side-by-side, it is apparent that they actually describe widely diverse realities. First of all, they do not even have the same genus of their definition: one is a kind of natural, moral union, while the other is a kind of artificial, legal contract. Secondly, they differ as to their ultimate cause: one is ultimately for the purpose of begetting children and raising them, the other is for the purpose of satisfying the wills of the persons involved. These considerations manifest that the likenesses between these two realities are quite superficial, while their differences are important. Therefore, there is good reason to hold that the same name should not be given to both of these widely diverse realities. Nevertheless, the discriminating reader will likely have some questions, or perhaps even serious objections to some of the assertions made here. If this is the case, I point you to the end of this chapter where I hope to consider the most significant objections that may arise.

NEW USES OF THE WORD "FAMILY"

With new uses of the word "marriage" come new uses of the word "family," for family is defined in terms of marriage. First of all, "family" in the new sense is essentially a man-made, legal reality instead of a natural, moral reality. This is because the cause of this new sense of "family" is not the natural ability and inclination to generate children, but rather the will of the individual persons involved. Since the new use of the term "marriage" includes any two persons who have romantic love for each other, it is clear that the term "family" can be used to refer to these "married" persons and any children they might legally adopt. And since there is nothing particularly significant about romantic love if it has no bearing on procreation, there is no reason why the state should give legal preference to those who have romantic love over those who do not. And so, if the state chooses, it can create a legal entity which it defines as a family based upon whatever criteria seem suitable. Thus, for example, a "family" can be defined as any number of persons who wish to have legal rights (such as inheritance rights and the right to act on behalf of one another) conferred upon their union by the state. Clearly, according to the new definition of "family," the state has absolute authority over the relationships within such a "family." Once again, family in the original sense of the word signifies something widely diverse from "family" in this new sense; and, therefore, there is good reason not to give these different realities the same name.

POSTSCRIPT

At the beginning of this book, I mentioned that there may be those who disagree strongly with the definitions of marriage and family I have proposed. For some people, the primary reason for this is because of some misunderstanding (for example, those who falsely thought that if marriage is for the sake of children then it is impossible for infertile couples to marry). I hope that the following objections and answers will address those concerns. But it is well known that disagreements are not solely the result of defects in the understanding. Sometimes disagreements occur because of negative experiences and associations. Thus it is entirely possible that one source of disagreement about the definition of family I have proposed springs from someone's personal negative experiences with their own family. Those who had an abusive or neglectful father or mother might associate the abuse or neglect with that parent, so that they might think that having a father or mother at all is a bad thing. On the other hand, many people do not come from an intact family as I have described it, and because people sometimes do not want to admit their family was defective, they defend their own experience of family as normative, or at least not in any way defective. But even those who disagree with the definition of family I have proposed for these motives, often admit that they would have liked to have a family as I have described it. I hope, dear reader, that if you come from such a background, you will have an open mind to consider honestly the experiences and arguments I have given without allowing negative associations to interfere with your evaluation of them. The basis for the account of family I have given is not based upon power structures or means of controlling others, but upon what is best for children. It is not family based upon what men want, but upon what children want.

OBJECTIONS AND ANSWERS

You have been very patient, my good reader, during this whole exercise of distinguishing various uses and meanings of the words "marriage" and "family." Now it is time to consider some of the most serious difficulties with the original definitions of marriage and family I have given above.

Objection 1: Elderly and infertile couples are unable to beget children, but everyone admits that they can marry. Therefore, marriage cannot be for the sake of generating children. And if infertile couples can marry, for the same reason, persons of the same sex can marry.

Answer: Even for infertile couples marriage is for the sake of generating children. Take a parallel example: a blind eye is still *for the sake of seeing*, even if it is *unable to see*. To be "for the sake of something" is not to be identified with what something is "able to do." In fact, we would never call something "broken" if we did not see this obvious distinction. Something is broken when it is *for the sake* of doing something, but is *unable* to do it. We would never call a hammer that could not calculate "broken" since it is not for the sake of calculating. But a calculator that cannot calculate is broken because it is for the sake of calculating.

To use a simple example, an infertile orange tree is for the sake of producing oranges, even if it is unable to produce them. And infertile marriage is for the sake of producing children even if it is unable to produce them. A sign that this is true is the fact that even the marriage of infertile couples involves sexual love (two people just living in the same house without any agreement about sexual intercourse are not married!). Nor would any intelligent person identify the inability of an infertile couple to generate children with the inability of a same-sex couple to generate children. The term "inability" in those two cases is used equivocally. No one wonders what is wrong with a same-sex couple when they haven't generated children after five years together. They are unable to generate children because they are *not supposed* to be able to generate children. So in the case of an infertile couple "unable to generate children" means an *impeded* natural ability, while in the case of the same-sex couple, "unable to generate children" means *no* natural ability (in fact, no ability of any kind). To identify the two would be like saying an infertile dog is the same as an orange tree, since both are unable to have puppies.

Moreover, because of this difference between infertile couples and same-sex couples, they should not be treated equally. No one thinks that an infertile dog is equivalent to an orange tree because neither of them can produce puppies. The infertile dog has a natural aptitude to produce puppies, even if some sickness prevents this. An orange tree has absolutely no natural aptitude to produce puppies. In the same way an infertile couple has a natural aptitude to produce children, but two persons of the same gender have absolutely no natural aptitude to produce children. If someone said to you: "this dog is infertile: we should treat it the same way we treat my orange tree which also cannot have puppies," you would see the obvious fallacy. Similarly, if someone says: "this man and woman are infertile, we should treat them as if they were the same as a man and a man who also cannot have children," we would see the obvious fallacy. Just as a dog that doesn't bear puppies still needs to be cared for in the manner keeping with its kind, so also sexual relations need to be respected according to their nature whether or not a child actually comes from them.

Objection 2: But if we say that marriage is for the sake of begetting children, doesn't that mean that an infertile couple are not married in the true sense of the word?

Answer: No. The whole definition of marriage is present in the case of an infertile couple. Just as a dog which cannot have puppies is still fully a dog, lacking nothing of the definition of dog, so an infertile couple that cannot have children are fully married. "Having children" is not in the definition of marriage. Rather "for the sake of begetting children" is in the definition of marriage.

Objection 3: But if someone knows they are infertile, it seems impossible for them to intend to enter into a marriage which they think is for the sake of begetting children.

Answer: Someone who knows they are infertile can still knowingly choose to enter into marriage, even though marriage is for the sake of the generation and education of children. A similar case might help explain. Let us say that a man wants to buy and get into a car. He knows that cars are for the sake of driving, and yet perhaps he does not even know how to drive a car (maybe he is a car collector, and just wants to buy it as an investment, and he just likes to sit in the car but doesn't want to drive it or can't drive it). Does it follow from the fact that cars are for the sake of driving that it is impossible for someone who can't drive to choose to buy and get into a car? Of course not. Even if the car itself isn't able to drive (maybe it's out of gas), the one who buys it is still choosing to buy a car. The car, in itself, is for the sake of driving regardless of the motives or abilities of the person who wants to buy it. Similarly, it is possible for someone who can't generate children to choose to get into something which is for the sake of generating children. So long as he intends to give to his spouse the exclusive right over his body for acts apt to generate children, he is entering into something which, in itself, is for the sake of generating children. His own motives or inabilities don't change that.[5]

---

5   On the other hand, if someone did not have even the ability for acts apt to generate children (for example, if they are missing their entire reproductive

Objection 4: Many if not most people marry for the sake of love, not primarily for the sake of children. In fact, some couples do not intend to have children at all when they marry. Therefore, marriage cannot be for the sake of begetting and educating children.

Answer: The first distinction that needs to be made is the distinction between *intrinsic purpose* and *motive*: the purpose of a thing may be different from the motive that people have in using or making it. The purpose of medicine is to heal, but the motive why some doctor uses or learns medicine could simply be making money. The making of money is not the purpose of medicine, and that would be so even if most doctors practiced medicine for the sake of making money. *To determine the intrinsic purpose of something one needs to look at its intrinsic structure and order.* The things a doctor learns when he goes to medical school, the experience he acquires, etc., are all ordered to becoming someone who can heal. In fact, if doctors began studying how to maximize profits as the primary purpose of their studies, eventually the medical art would be destroyed, since producing health would take a back seat to making money (for example, doctors would not study or use the things that most of all contribute to health, but rather things that most of all contributed to their profits).

Applying this distinction to marriage, it may be true that the motive most people have for marrying in our culture is love, but that does not mean that the intrinsic purpose of marriage is not the generation and education of children. People can love one another in various ways, but marriage involves sexual love and therefore is, in itself, ordered to the generation of children (even if no children happen to come about). So long as the couple understands that they are giving to each other the lifelong and exclusive right over one another's body for acts apt to generate children, then they have chosen something which has the generation of children as its intrinsic purpose: i.e., they have given the consent necessary for marriage, even if their primary motive for choosing to marry is love. If that

---

organ), then they could not enter into a marriage, since then they could not honestly give to someone else the right for acts apt to generate children.

consent be lacking, there is no marriage. So if someone attempts to marry, but does so positively excluding the right of the other to use their ability to generate children, there is no marriage.

Objection 5: Why isn't love in the definition of marriage? Most people agree that marriage is for love.

Answer: In some measure love is implied in three parts of the definition: *communion, freely consenting and for the sake of begetting and educating children*. Would you want to have a child with just anyone? Or be bound to live the rest of your life with just anyone? That love is required for a *good* marriage is therefore evident from the definition. But notice: what makes something good is not necessarily in the definition of that thing: virtue makes a man good, but virtue is not in the definition of man. Health makes an animal good, but health is not in the definition of animal. Similarly, love makes a marriage good, but love is not in the definition of marriage.

That being said, a distinction should be made between emotional love and the choice to love: that is, the will to act for the good of another. Emotional love is often not in our control, and so it is not reasonable to expect that emotional love should be in the definition of marriage. If it were, marriage would have no stability at all and could hardly be called a union or a communion. Even with regard to the choice to love, the definition of marriage should not imply that if two people don't love each other anymore, then their marriage is over, and they are free to move on. Love does not make marriage *to be*, but *to be good*. So the existence of marriage does not depend upon love, even if the goodness of a marriage does. However, as implied by the three elements of the definition of marriage mentioned above, intention to love one another seems to be required for a marriage to come into existence.[6]

---

6   Notice that the cause of a thing's coming into existence is not always the same as the cause of a thing's existence. Your parents are the causes of your coming into existence, but they are not the causes of your existence. Otherwise when they died so would you! Similarly, the intention to will the good of your spouse may be required for the coming into existence of the marriage, but the marriage does not cease to exist if that choice to love is absent at some time

Objection 6: Marriage is not necessarily lifelong. Many people get divorced and remarried several times, and society recognizes their marriages as true marriages. Besides, if the spouses cause their marriage to be, they can also cause it not to be.

Answer: As I have already said above, since reason sees that human children ought to be not only begotten, but also loved and educated by their own parents, lifelong communion between spouses is something demanded by human nature for its perfection. The natural inclinations which indicate what is needed for human perfection reveal that the particular kind of relationship which provides for begetting children must be lifelong in order to fulfill those natural inclinations. Here the descriptive term *lifelong* means that the spouses must *intend* to remain united for their entire lives at the time they marry. If this is lacking, then the union would not be a marriage properly speaking. Moreover one can see from other parts of the definition of marriage why it has to be lifelong. For if marriage is *for the sake of the education of children*, it is clear that this is substantially a lifelong common activity. Even parents of grown children continue to educate their grown children by providing an example of how to live virtuously in the next stage of their lives. Finally, because marriage is a kind of *communion*, it must also be lifelong. For communion implies oneness of life, and nobody wants to live only part of their own life. So too, one who shares the life of another in communion wants to share the whole of their life. Even a good friendship should be lifelong, all the more so should marriage be lifelong. Without this it would not be a true communion. So from all three of these considerations, we can see that marriage demands a lifelong communion. And this is not because of some extrinsic imposition by the mere will of those who enter into marriage: it is demanded by what marriage is in itself; it is intrinsic to the nature of marriage.

Exceptions where people don't seem inclined to care for their own children only prove the rule. For example, abusive parents who abandon or seriously harm their children are recognized as failures

---

later on in one or both of the spouses.

in parenting. If there was no compelling reason why parents should raise their own children together, we would not blame parents who chose not to.

As to the objection that society recognizes second and third marriages after divorce, since marriage is something natural rather than something artificial, the definition of marriage does not depend upon social agreement (though designating one word rather than another to refer to this natural reality does depend upon social agreement, as in English we say "marriage," but in Italian "matrimonio"). In fact, even in societies where divorce and remarriage is common, the implicit assumption is that marriage is supposed to be lifelong. For example, even in civil marriages, the presumption is that the persons intend to remain with the same person for the rest of their life. Otherwise, why would the law automatically grant inheritance rights to the spouse? Moreover, there is no provision made for a marriage which automatically terminates after some set time period. To have a marriage declared over by the state, the persons have to go through a civil divorce. So these are signs that even in society as a whole the concept of marriage is something that *should be* lifelong.

Finally, the fact that the spouses cause their marriage to exist does not mean that they can cause their marriage to cease to exist. Someone can be the cause of a thing's existence without being a cause of its continued existence. Parents cause their children to come into existence, but they are not directly responsible for the continued existence of their children. Both parents might even die, and the children will still exist. Nor does the fact that the parents caused the existence of their children give them the right to cause their children not to exist! Moreover, when a child comes into existence, a moral obligation also comes into existence at the same time: the moral obligation of the parent to love and care about the child and the moral obligation of the child to honor its parents. The parents can cause this moral obligation to come to be, but they cannot cause it to end: they are always obliged to love and care about their children. Similarly, spouses can cause their marriage to be, but they cannot end their marriages.

Objection 7: Two people should be free to choose to marry and then choose not to be married, especially when there is abuse by one of the spouses.

Answer: In every marriage, there is a grave obligation to do everything in one's power to remain together and to love one another. Human frailty and disordered emotions do not absolve one from the responsibility to acknowledge one's own faults, to repent, and to take responsibility for one's own actions. Marriage is not an artificial creation of the human mind or will, it is the object of a natural inclination which perfects us as human beings. Leaving one's spouse is never, in itself, perfective of human nature and so cannot lead to true happiness. If marriage is difficult for one or both spouses, this is not because marriage itself is harmful to them. The marriage is not the problem, so divorce is not the solution. The real problem is some lack of virtue in one or both spouses, and it is that problem which needs to be addressed. The person who divorces to get out of the pain they feel in their marriage is like the person who decides to stop eating because his tooth is hurting him. Eating in itself is not the problem (in fact, it is perfective of our nature). The real problem is his sick tooth, and that needs to be healed if his nature is to be perfected. So the person who escapes his problems by divorce is not really helping himself, he's actually hurting himself by ignoring the true problem.

This being said, the case of serious abuse by one of the spouses is a reason to separate physically from the spouse and even a reason to take legal action to ensure support from that spouse if that is necessary. But it is not a reason to consider oneself free to remarry.

Objection 8: Same-sex couples do just as good a job raising children as male and female couples. Therefore, there is no good reason to restrict marriage to persons of the opposite sex.

Answer: Marriage is not defined by how good a job adults do in raising the children. The definition of marriage does not include the expression "where both persons do a good job raising the children." For that matter, a brother and sister might do a good job raising the children of their deceased sibling, but for all that, this does not justify their getting married.

Moreover, the premise that same-sex couples do just as good a job raising children can clearly be shown to be false both empirically and from sound reasoning. Serious studies on the matter have shown the grave harm that has come to children raised by same-sex couples.[7] More importantly, no one needs a study to see the obvious truth that women cannot be good fathers or that men cannot be good mothers. To be a good father and mother are intrinsically linked to one's sex. Children adopted by a homosexual couple will be deprived of a father or mother. Imagine growing up never knowing at all what it is like to have a father, or what it is like to have a mother? You don't have to be a psychologist to notice that relationships between the sexes later on in life are largely determined by the original parent-child relationship. Girls who had bad relationships or experiences with their fathers, for example, tend to have bad relationships with their boyfriends and husbands later on in life. Similarly boys with their mothers. Furthermore, the primary example which a child follows to learn how to be a fully developed man or woman is from their parent of the same sex. If there is a defect in that relationship, they usually have to find a father figure or mother figure to heal the wound. Moreover, the children have no example of a relationship between a husband and wife. When people marry, the first and best way they judge how to relate to their spouse is by imitating their parents and remembering how they interacted.

Also, by giving children to homosexual couples, the state is making a public judgment that mothers are expendable (since two men do just as well) and that fathers are expendable (since two women do just as well). In other words, the society teaches children that fathers and mothers give nothing unique, essential or irreplaceable to family

---

7   It is true that there are many studies which claim that same-sex couples raise children as well as heterosexual couples. But any educated person is aware that studies, like polls and statistics, can easily be manipulated to generate a predetermined result. In a society where those in power are promoting same-sex unions, this is especially likely. Therefore, no one should accept the evidence of a study (regardless of its conclusions) without carefully evaluating its methodology and statistical value (for example, the sample size must be large enough to eliminate bias).

life. This is clearly harmful to the common good and contrary to truth and common sense. Finally, giving children an example of sexual intimacy between two persons of the same sex is not raising them well.[8]

Objection 9: Marriage is not something natural, but rather something man-made. It's obvious that the consent of the spouses makes the marriage.

Answer: While this or that marriage comes into existence by the consent of the spouses, what marriage is does not come to be by their consent. Similarly, the existence of this or that human being is caused by its parents, but what it is to be human (human nature) is not caused by any two parents.

If someone were to say that just as men make chairs or cars to be what they are, so too, the very "what it is to be marriage" is something man-made, there is much clear evidence that marriage is natural. We can show this step by step.

First, the human desire to sexually reproduce is natural. For any good which human nature cannot be or be well without, is a good to which human nature is inclined. But reproduction of our species is clearly such. Therefore we have a natural desire to reproduce. Moreover, it seems that everyone admits that the desire for sexual pleasure is natural. But nature provides pleasures and desires as enticements to perform the activities necessary for the being and well-being of our nature. For example, the pleasure associated with eating is an enticement to get us to nourish our bodies, and the desire to sleep is an enticement to replenish our bodies, and the desire to breathe is an enticement to provide our bodies with necessary oxygen, etc. Clearly, the desire for sexual intercourse is for the sake of the goods which ordinarily result from sexual intercourse. It is obvious that among the goods which ordinarily result from sexual activity is children. In fact, children are the greatest good that results from sexual activity. Ask any parent, which is better: their child or the pleasure they experienced in conceiving that child?

8 This assertion will be defended in the following chapters.

So the desire to generate children must be natural: the very name "nature" is derived from a Latin word meaning birth, so what could be more natural than giving birth? The second step to manifest that marriage as we have defined it is natural is to see that remaining in a stable union with someone we have children with is natural. This is obvious because it is natural to desire to live with and care for our own children. Our children are like an extension of ourselves. And we naturally care for them like our own bodies. If we did not, our species would die out. Moreover, since every child has two parents, and each of them wants to live with and raise their own child, it follows that it is natural to want to live together with the other parent of our child, and to raise that child with their other parent. A sign of this is the strong emotional bonds which form between a man and woman who have intercourse.

The next step is to see that monogamy is natural. Whatever is necessary to contribute to the being or well-being of human nature is natural. But having only one spouse (monogamy) contributes to the well-being of human nature. Therefore, monogamy is natural. It is obvious that having only one spouse contributes to the well-being of human nature. If a woman had many husbands, there would be no natural way for the men to know which child was theirs, and so they would not have as strong a desire to care for the children from that union. On the other hand, if a man had many wives, there would likely be more children than the husband could care for morally and physically. Raising a human child requires living with the child for many years, and making great sacrifices of time & energy. Having more than one spouse and set of children divides our attention and weakens the bonds of love and friendship. Besides, the wives would be unequal to the husband, and loved with only half his heart, if that. As a consequence, the children would feel loved only in part by their father. There would also be the constant fear that the father would begin to prefer one wife over another and one set of children over another. There are many signs which confirm the fact that monogamy is natural. First of all, there are the natural jealousies which arise when one man is desired by many women, or one woman is desired by many men. Secondly, there is the fact that in our species, men and women are born in roughly equal numbers, unlike other species (such as lions) where there are multiple females born for every male. Finally, there is the fact that a single woman can produce about as many children as a man could reasonably raise and care for. So there is no need for a man to marry several women in order to ensure the continuation of our species.

Finally, we can see that it is natural for the marriage bond to be publicly recognized and defended. Only in this way can their lifelong bond be respected by others in the community, so that adultery will be less common. Besides, it is harder to back out of a public commitment than a private one. And just as a cast is helpful to heal a broken leg, so also external social pressure and the expectation that people keep public promises is helpful for broken marriages. A marriage which might have failed due to lack of sufficient time to heal might heal in a society where it is expected that the spouses stay together and work on their marriage. In a world full of broken legs, it is important that there be casts; in a world full of broken marriages, it is important that there be social pressure keeping marriages together until they can properly heal. In summary, human beings discover in their own natures that the only reasonable and responsible way to bring their children into the world is when one man and one woman come together for life in order to have and raise children, and do so by their mutual consent made known to a community. In other words, marriage is natural.

Objection 10: Different people have different natural desires, so each one should be able to determine for himself what kind of marriage and family fulfill those desires.

Answer: This objection is due to a confusion about the meaning of the expression "natural desire" or "natural inclination." A natural desire or inclination is not the same as a conscious desire, though conscious desires are often the sign or effect of natural desires. When I feel some emotion, or am aware of wanting some good, then I am experiencing a conscious desire. In contrast, a natural desire is not something necessarily felt or willed: it is an inclination of the nature itself for its perfection. For example, a plant is naturally inclined to grow and bear fruit and reproduce; an animal is naturally inclined to develop the organs needed for its perfect activity (as when a dog embryo grows eyes and teeth). These examples manifest that natural inclinations are not always accompanied by a conscious desire. But sometimes natural inclinations are accompanied by conscious desires. Because our nature is such that it needs food and water and air to exist, there are natural inclinations for these things. So we can define a natural inclination or "desire" as the tendency a natural thing has for the activities necessary to preserve that nature in existence. In a secondary sense, a natural inclination or "desire" is a tendency for the activities necessary for the well-being of that nature.

Now, since there is one human nature common to us all, it follows from this that there cannot be different natural desires for different men, since natural desire is defined above as an inclination of the nature itself which all men have in common.

Corresponding to these natural inclinations are also conscious desires (hunger, thirst, the desire to breathe). Since these conscious desires are for goods necessary to perfect our nature, they are often called natural as well. So when we speak about a natural conscious desire we don't mean just any desire that someone is born with, or a desire that someone can't choose not to have. Indeed, there might be some desires that are contrary to the perfection of our nature, yet those who have them can't choose to not have them. The desire to kill ourselves or others, the desire for harmful drugs or alcohol, the desire to molest a child, the desire to commit incest, etc., might in some cases be such that the person who has them can't choose to feel otherwise. Yet it is clear that such desires do not perfect our nature. As we have shown above, the inclination to reproduce and the inclination to form a communion with a spouse and children are clearly inclinations of our nature. And the conscious desires which usually result from these natural inclinations are also natural in some sense. But any haphazard conscious desire (even one that can't be changed) is not sufficient to form a marriage or a family.

That being said, if a desire is natural, it will usually be accompanied by a corresponding conscious desire. For if that were not the case, the nature would not obtain what it needs for perfection. Unless some natural inclinations were accompanied by conscious desires in animals, the individuals would soon die or be gravely harmed, and the species would die out.

Objection 11: Even if there are some differences between a marriage between a man and a woman and a same-sex union, practically speaking treating them as equivalent does no harm.

Answer: Different things should not be treated as if they are equal precisely in the respect in which they are different. This is all the more true when the differences are significant, and when we are considering such a basic element of human life as marriage and family.

A simple example will suffice to illustrate. If a grocer put out tomatoes and round red rocks in the same bin and calls them all tomatoes, he has treated different things as if they were equal. Someone might respond: well they are equal insofar as they are round and red. True, but the grocer is treating them as if they were both fruit, when they are not. Precisely in the respect in which they are different, he is treating them as if they were equal.

Similarly, it is wrong and deceptive to treat marriage as equal to the legal unions contracted by persons of the same-sex. True, there are some similarities: two persons are involved, and they desire to stimulate their reproductive organs with one another, and the union is recognized by law. But those similarities do not make marriage any more than red and round make tomatoes.

First of all, marriage is between a man and a woman. Same-sex unions are between a man and a man or a woman and a woman. This may be obvious, but it is a difference, and a very significant difference. Men and women are not alike biologically (even their brains are significantly different), psychologically or emotionally. The tremendous amount of research detailing the many significant differences between men and women only serves to confirm what everyone already knew: men and women are not interchangeable. So relationships between men and women will not be identical to relationships between men and men or women and women. Without even making a judgment about one being better or worse than the other, the stark fact remains: they are significantly different, so they should not be treated as if they were the same.

Secondly, marriage is not essentially a legal contract created by the state. Marriage is a lifelong communion of a man and woman, established by their free consent, for the sake of the generation and education of children. This communion is a *moral union*, not a *legal contract*. Moreover, marriage in the sense just defined clearly existed before any state existed. Families existed first, then tribes, then villages. By the time written laws came around, they were simply made to recognize marriage, not to create it. So marriage is something *natural predating the state*, while same-sex unions are something *artificial created by the state*.

Thirdly, marriage is different from same-sex unions because it is for the sake of generating children. The fact that both a heterosexual couple and a same-sex couple intend to use their reproductive organs with each other attempts to treat them as equal in the very respect in which they are different. Reproductive organs are (not surprisingly) for reproduction. The male and female of one species each have half of the single reproductive organ for the species. Only together can either one generate children. Two males or two females of the same species can in no way be said to be attempting to reproduce, that is, to fulfill the purpose of their reproductive organs. So the ability to reproduce is precisely the way in which a heterosexual couple and a homosexual couple are different. To treat them as equal is patently false. No one would ever claim that a same-sex union was for the sake of generating children. But that is exactly what marriage is for.

So looking back we can see that there are five major differences between same-sex unions and marriage: 1) Marriage is between a man and a woman, which constitutes a major difference from a relationship between a man and a man or a woman and a woman; 2) Marriage is natural, same-sex unions are artificial; 3) Marriage predates civil authority, same-sex unions are created by civil authority; 4) Marriage is a moral union, same-sex unions are legal unions; 5) Marriage is for the sake of generating children, same-sex unions have nothing to do with generating children. To insist on giving them the same name, and treating them as equal is clearly foolish and wrong (even if you have no moral objections to homo-sexual activity).

Objection 12: Even if marriage is not the same as same-sex unions, they are similar enough to be treated as equal under the law. For example, persons of different skin color are not the same, but those differences are not legally significant, so they should be treated as equal under the law.

Answer: One of the purposes of law is to ensure that people are treated fairly. Therefore, when differences between things require that they be treated different in order to be fair, these differences are legally significant as well. We noted above that marriage differs from same-sex unions in many ways: 1) because relationships between men and women are different than relationships between persons of the same sex; 2) because marriage is natural and pre-dates the state, while same-sex unions are created by the state; and 3) because marriage is for the sake of the generation and educa-tion of children.

(1) A relationship between a man and a woman should not be treated the same under law as a relationship between persons of the same sex. For example, in a domestic abuse case between a husband and wife, the legal presumption should be in favor of the defense of the woman (even if she provokes the conflict) because a man is morally obliged to protect his wife (this presumption is also at the root of why men but not women can be drafted into the military). But if the union is between two men or two women, the law should treat them equally, without a presumption that one ought to protect the other. Therefore, it would not be fair to women to treat marriage between a man and a woman the same as a union between persons of the same sex. Moreover, since hav-ing a father and a mother is better for a child than not having a father or mother, and same-sex unions cannot provide both, then it is not fair to children to treat these unions as legally equivalent. Thus, for example, the law should treat same-sex unions differ-ently from marriage in regard to adoption of children.

(2) Natural entities such as persons, marriage, family, and gender (male and female) ought to be treated differently under law than artificial entities created by the state such as legal contracts and corporate structures. Natural things are not social constructs, nor does their dignity arise from or depend upon the state. To the contrary, the state has a duty to recognize and foster natural entities which are presupposed to the good of the state, and does not have the authority to manipulate such entities. To exercise authority over natural things is a mark of a totalitarian state. Thus, the state does not exercise unlimited authority over marriage: because the state does not cause marriage, aspects of marriage fall outside the authority of the state. On the contrary, the state has the right to redefine and change at will artificial entities created by the state as needed for public expediency. Therefore, it would not be fair to treat marriage the same as same-sex unions.

(3) Finally, a relationship which is in itself ordered to the generation and education of children obviously stands in a different relationship to the common good of the state than a relationship that is ordered to emotional satisfaction. The state depends upon new children in a more radical way than it depends upon emotionally satisfied citizens. For example, a relationship which is for the sake of the generation and education of children demands more stability than a relationship which is for emotional satisfaction, and so it would not be fair to deprive marriage of the legal protections which promote greater stability. Besides, not everything that is for the sake of emotional satisfaction promotes the common good. For example, both adultery and heroin use are sought for emotional satisfaction. Thus, not every relationship ordered to emotional satisfaction deserves the protection of law.

Objection 13: No harm is done to you if I decide to have a family different from your concept of family. You still have the right to marry as you always did.

Answer: First of all, what is at stake here is not merely one group of people deciding to have different relationships than another group of persons in the privacy of their homes. What is at stake here is a change in the law and the public views propagated in a whole society. So it is patently false to claim that no one else is being affected. Everyone in that society is necessarily affected. Not only that, but the change in society that is being proposed is a radically different concept of family and marriage. Even a very simple person can see that this entails a complete reordering of society which affects every member in that society in matters that are extremely important and personal. To change what everyone means by family is to change everyone's family life in a radical way.

Secondly, it is possible to hurt someone in more ways than by physical damage. For example, denying someone an education or access to important truths necessary for their human perfection hurts them. Denying someone the healthy human relationships that they need to flourish hurts them. The following is a list of different ways in which persons can be hurt in a society that redefines marriage and family.

(1) First, someone can hurt themselves by acting in such a way that fails to appreciate the goodness of the natural order. (For those who know or believe that God exists, this is especially important, since access to the beauty and wisdom of the mind of God as revealed through creation is lost: and this is the most important education of all). When someone does not see the purpose of procreation and the need for the natural family as the right context for a reproductive act, they fail to understand the great good involved in cooperating with that natural order. The goodness of the natural family itself becomes obscured. Anyone who is married and is raising children knows how difficult this is. Unless people in a society see clearly the good of the natural family and of children in particular, they will not, on the whole, be willing to make the great sacrifices necessary to form stable families and raise children. Why would you do something very difficult if you saw very little good in it? As a consequence, divorce proliferates and the population begins to decrease beyond sustainable levels. Eventually, a whole nation or people dies out (as happened to ancient Rome, and is happening to several modern nations). So society at large is harmed by the mindset that accepts an understanding of the family which is incompatible with human nature.

(2) Second, when society begins to accept that homosexual acts are morally acceptable, and that a union of persons based upon such acts is equal to a natural family, such same-sex unions claim the right to have children (which children obviously come from a mother and father, who are the natural parents of those children). These children are then raised without a father or without a mother: that is a grave injustice to those children. It is one thing when because of circumstances beyond anyone's control a child is deprived of a father or mother, but it is an entirely different thing to do this on purpose. The natural consequence of this is that children will be taught that every member of a family is expendable and unnecessary: if two moms can do just as good a job as a mother and father, then society is saying that the father is useless and expendable. If two dads can do just as good a job as a father and a mother, then society is teaching that the mother is expendable and useless. Moreover, not only will these children be raised without a father or without a mother, the couple who are raising them will be in an expressly homosexual relationship, so that the children will grow up being told that sexual love and activity between persons of the same sex is morally good.

(3) Third, in a society where homosexual unions are treated as equal to marriage, the children will necessarily be constantly told by the society that this is true. So even in families with a father and mother who do not agree that same-sex couples can marry, they will have their parents telling them one thing and the society telling them something else (with the compulsive force of law I might add, so that the schools will be forced to teach this position). Children will be harmed because this causes confusion and distrust of authority (since the authorities will necessarily contradict on a very important matter). Not only that but many of the children's peers and friends will hold this false position, and to hold true to their own position they will be forced to break off many peer relationships which are necessary for healthy human development. Keeping one's children out of society is no solution since that also causes grave harm to children. Moreover, any attempt to explain homosexual unions as if they were marriage will necessarily lead to a discussion of homosexual sex, which will corrupt the innocence

of children. The past few years have exposed the false assertions of those who claimed that making same-sex unions legally equivalent to marriage will not affect families who disagree.

(4) Fourth, in addition to the children, adults in the society will be harmed because many will adopt a false view about marriage. Many adults are not sufficiently educated to see with certitude and clarity what is good and bad. For example, if you were to ask an average adult "what makes an action good or bad?" or "what is the definition of the term 'good'?" It is unlikely that they could give a carefully thought out answer to these important questions. They depend upon others to help them. So if the powerful in society introduce ways of thinking through social communication, many people will simply adopt the positions they are used to hearing. If the history of the past century has proven anything, it is that propaganda works. Communism, Fascism, and many instances of genocide were largely caused by propaganda. There is no reason to believe that false positions about marriage cannot be disseminated in the same way. When a large portion of society accepts the false view that same-sex unions are equated with marriage, this leads to errors about married life. For example, it will sever the connection between marriage and children in many people's minds. In many people's minds, marriage becomes a state-created vehicle to make it easier to fulfill sexual drives and needs rather than for accomplishing goods (i.e., begetting children). If that is what marriage is, then why should it be lifelong? As soon as your drive or sexual need is no longer being satisfied by this partner, then there is no reason for the marriage to exist, and the state will be very happy to supply you with another partner. This is bad for marriage and obviously for families. Children are always the ones who will suffer the most when marriage is misunderstood.

(5) Fifth, the natural family is something that precedes the state: natural families existed long before any civil societies did. Same-sex "marriages" are created by the state, and can only continue to exist if constantly supported by the state. When same-sex "marriage" is made equal to natural marriage the state begins to treat natural marriage and family as if they were the property and creation of the

state too. The state will then begin to exercise authority that it does not legitimately possess over families and marriages. In such a state, the duty to recognize and protect marriage and the family turns into a right to manipulate marriage and family. This is a mark of a totalitarian state: it's inability to admit that some things (especially natural things) fall outside of its power, and the unwillingness to abide by the principle of subsidiarity (i.e., the principle that certain goods, such as moral education of children, are more perfectly attained by subsidiary groups, such as families).

(6) Sixth, any definition of marriage which excludes reference to reproduction will necessarily lead to many other kinds of state sanctioned relationships that are also harmful to children. What does "marriage" mean when applied to persons of the same sex? A natural marriage is easily definable in terms of its natural purpose: marriage is a lifelong communion of a man and woman, established by their free consent, for the sake of the generation and education of children. But for persons of the same sex, the definition must be something like "a state recognized legal union between persons who desire to enjoy sexual pleasure together." If the purpose of such unions is to enjoy sexual pleasure together, then why should they be limited to two people? And why couldn't members of the same family, like a father and a son get "married" since they are as capable of enjoying sexual pleasure as any other two people? With natural marriage it is clear that things like polygamy and incest harm the education of the children, so they would be excluded. But there seems to be no reason to exclude such things according to the new definition of marriage. After all, if marriage is utterly unrelated to procreation and raising children what reasonable limits could one place upon the kinds of relationships that could constitute such a "marriage"? Someone might object that the enjoyment of sexual relations is not important for same-sex unions, but if that is the case, then practically any friendship could be called marriage: marriage is not just friendship. From these considerations it can be seen that the acceptance of the alternate definitions of marriage and family given above harms society in many ways.

This concludes the objections and answers to the definitions of marriage and family I have given above. Other frequently asked questions are included in Appendix I at the end of the book. Certainly other questions still remain: questions about human nature, and following reason; questions about the morality of reproductive acts, etc. I did not intend to address those issues here. The purpose of this section was simply to lay out and defend definitions of marriage and family in such a way as to see 1) how these definitions describe something real in human experience; and 2) how they differ in important ways from other definitions of these words which have recently been proposed. In the next chapter I will set forth some principles by which we can judge whether marriage and family (according to the different definitions proposed today) are good or bad.

2

Reason and Nature as Sources of Moral Standards

IN THE LAST CHAPTER, I CONSIDERED THE DEFI-
nitions of marriage and family and how these definitions are rooted
in human nature as apprehended by reason. At this point, I intend
to consider human nature and reason as sources of moral standards
in matters pertaining to the family, that is, of right and wrong. This
raises a larger question: How can someone determine what is right
and wrong in human actions generally speaking (not just in matters pertaining to family life)? This chapter (and the next one on
choosing between apparently conflicting goods) lays down principles
which are broader than marriage and family life. However they are
included because many of the objections against marriage and family
are actually broader objections against morality as such. However, in
order not to distract needlessly from the main theme of this work, I
will only lay down the basic principles needed to resolve the main
objections which are often raised today. Therefore, the next two
chapters should not be considered to be a comprehensive course
on ethics or morality.

Another caveat: some of the explanations in these next two chapters may go beyond the scope of what may be of interest to you, dear
reader. There is a lot of detail about terms like "nature," and many
of the arguments are about very universal and sometimes abstract
principles. I must consider these things, however, because they are
the ultimate areas of dispute, and no treatment of marriage or family
would be complete without them. Nevertheless, some readers may
find these chapters taxing and too philosophical. If you are among
them, then by all means, take what you find to be helpful in these
chapters, but do not feel that you cannot go on to the remainder

of this book without having mastered everything in these next two chapters. For those who want a more careful treatment of these universal principles, it is here for the taking. For those who find it tedious and too difficult, do not hesitate to leave aside those parts which are not helpful for you.

THE NEED FOR A SOURCE OF MORAL STANDARDS

How does someone judge whether an action is good or bad, right or wrong? Obviously, if we are to hold that some actions are right and others are wrong, there must be some standard we are using, at least implicitly. But what is this standard? Is it just what seems good to each person: what each individual wants? Is it civil law? Is it the customs with which we were raised? Or is it something else? The fact that we judge certain actions to be right and others to be wrong is admitted by everyone. Let us take some examples. Feeding the poor, comforting the suffering, loving our children are clearly good actions. Starving the poor, torturing others and hating our children are clearly bad actions. It is easy enough to find clear cases in either category. But what about cases in between that are not obvious to everyone? Some people hold that it is sometimes good to view pornography, while some people hold the opposite. Some people hold that it is sometimes good to use contraception to prevent the conception of a child, while others hold the opposite. Some people say that it is sometimes good for persons of the same sex to be free to marry, while others say the opposite. Indeed, over the past 30 years, views have changed dramatically on these points, sometimes changing to the very opposite of what was held before. To make things even more complicated, what reason could be given why polygamy is wrong when the parties consent to them? Isn't the man who marries several women and divorces each of them and only supports his children with a check worse than the man who stays married to all his wives and tries to be present to the children from all his marriages? So for these cases which are not obvious to everyone, we need to answer the larger question: what makes an action or a choice good or bad?

ARE RIGHT AND WRONG COMPLETELY SUBJECTIVE?

One answer might be that while there is what is right and wrong for me and right and wrong for you, there is no such thing as an objective standard of right and wrong by which we must both abide. This position is commonly referred to as moral relativism or moral subjectivism. Setting aside for the moment the truth or falsity of this position, one thing is clear: since many of our actions bear upon others and, therefore, come into conflict with others, then when there is a conflict, the individual or group which is more powerful will determine which action is to be done. For example, if I think it is my right to have this piece of pizza, and you think it is your right, then, since there is no objective standard to which we are both subject, then the pizza will go to the one who has more power to take it. Moral relativism necessarily leads to conflict and oppression of the weak (which is why it is a philosophy held not by the weak but by the oppressing class). Moreover, those who get what they want by force do not experience happiness, which is another sure sign that this account of morality is defective.

Investigating the truth of the matter further, there are many reasons which clearly show moral relativism to be a false account of the standards of morality. The first thing to observe is that a person's beliefs are manifested more by his actions than his words. Someone might say that whatever you think is good for you is right for you, but no one acts like he believes this when he or someone he loves is getting hurt. No one can stand by as their child is being murdered or their wife being raped, and honestly think that this is morally good for the murderer or the rapist to do this. If someone claims otherwise, he is a liar: he doesn't believe his own words.

The second thing to observe is that according to moral subjectivism, there is no difference between a real good and an apparent good: the good by definition is the one which is apparent at the time you choose it, what seems good to you. If the good is whatever someone wants, and no one can fail to want what he wants when he wants it, then it is impossible to choose an apparent good and not a real one. Yet it is part of obvious moral experience that some goods we seek are real and others only apparent, which we later realize were not truly good after all.

Third, good or right seem to have no intelligible meaning for one who claims that whatever someone wants is good and right. When someone holds that it is "good" to hate all men, to murder and rape, simply because by "good" he means "whatever anyone chooses," this reveals that he is using the word "good" contrary to the actual meaning of the word.

Again, if whatever someone wants is automatically good for them, and since some people want to kill themselves, it would follow that destroying themselves would be necessarily good for them. But what does it mean to say that non-existence is a good for them? By destroying something or someone, you take away all good from them. It makes no sense to say that a non-existing thing has more goodness than an existing thing. Goodness doesn't belong to nothing! To use the word "good" that way simply empties it of any meaning whatsoever. It would be like saying that someone is enjoying himself after he doesn't exist: enjoyment doesn't belong to nothing, and neither does goodness. So it is clear that whatever someone wants is not necessarily good for them: the word good means what is perfective of someone, not what is destructive of someone.

Finally, the moral relativist cannot say that any action is bad in itself, or makes the person who does it bad. Therefore, there would be no reason to blame someone for their actions, nor would there be any reason for punishment. For punishment does not mean just harming someone for no reason, but it means harming them *in retribution for a fault*. But if there is no fault, there can be no punishment.

These difficulties reveal that the position that the good is completely subjective cannot account for moral experience nor can it serve as a basis for moral standards.

DO LAWS OR CUSTOMS DETERMINE RIGHT AND WRONG?

Another answer might be that whatever laws or social conventions are held by a given society are what determine what is considered good or bad. If a society accepts pornography, for example, then it should be considered good. This position has a certain appeal because of the common experience that the opinions of those around us strongly influence what we perceive as right and wrong.

However, this answer cannot be right. First of all, it is one thing to say that customs of a society influence *our perception* of right and wrong, it is quite another thing to say that the customs of society *determine what is in fact* right or wrong. The laws, customs and conventions of a society can influence the morality of actions in a limited way (for example, it might be considered rude not to bow in greeting in Japan, but not in the United States). Yet these laws or customs cannot completely determine which acts are right or wrong. It is true to say that *some* morals are determined by social conventions, but there is little evidence that *all* morals are determined by social conventions. It is obvious that some laws and customs of certain countries or cultures are bad. It is obvious, for example, that even if the vast majority of persons in a society held that it is right to exterminate all Jews, this would not make it right. It is obvious that even if the vast majority of a society held that all blacks should be slaves, this would not make it right. Exterminating Jews and enslaving blacks are bad uses of freedom no matter what the conventions of a society are (if these examples are not sufficiently convincing, rest assured even more obviously wrong social conventions can be imagined). Sometimes the views of a society, like Nazi Germany, are just corrupt and wrong.

Finally, if social customs determine right or wrong, this presupposes the objective moral standard that it is right to agree with others in your society and wrong to disagree with them. But why would that be? So even according to this theory, there seems to be an objective moral standard outside of the social customs themselves. So it is obvious that the laws or social conventions of a given society do not determine what is good or bad. There must be some more ultimate standard of right and wrong.

DOES NOT HURTING OTHERS DETERMINE RIGHT AND WRONG?

The above considerations have led many to posit that there must be some objective and universal moral standard for all men, but that this standard is merely that so long as our actions don't hurt anyone else they can be considered right. Let's investigate this answer: First let's look at reasons why it might be a right answer, then let's look at reasons that it might be a wrong answer.

Why should harm to others be the standard of the good or bad? Well, if I admit that besides myself others have freedom, and if it is good for me to use my freedom, then it is clear that it will be good for the others to also use their freedom. So for this reason, it seems right that I should be able to use my freedom so long as it doesn't keep others from using theirs. And since preventing another person from using their freedom harms them, it seems that the right use of freedom implies that freedom should be used in such a way that it doesn't hurt others. This general rule of human action might be formulated as: everyone should be free to do what they want so long as it doesn't hurt others or restrict their freedom.

But shouldn't the right use of freedom also demand that I don't hurt myself? To this someone could respond that whatever we freely choose we want, so that it is always good for us, even if other people think it hurts us: I can't impinge upon or restrict my own freedom.

On the other hand, there are reasons to think that not hurting others can't be the only standard by which we determine if our freedom is used well or badly. For example, it is a fact of experience that we sometimes are wrong about what is actually good for us and we regret it later. Taking addictive drugs seems good to many people when they start, and they do it freely, but then when they are addicted to them, they realize that it's really harming them and they want to stop but can't. Similarly, viewing pornography seems good, or at least harmless, to some people when they start, but when it becomes habitual and they begin to see its harmful effects, they want to stop and often can't. So it isn't true that we can never use our freedom to harm ourselves. And we certainly ought to love ourselves as much as our neighbor. So the right use of freedom seems to demand that we not only do no harm to others, but also that we do not harm ourselves.

Another question that comes up here is what does it mean to harm someone? Does it mean to cause them physical pain? Dentists and doctors have to cause physical pain to their patients sometimes, but we do not think that it is always wrong for them to do so. Parents sometimes have to punish their children, which often results in physical or emotional pain. But often these punishments turn out to be good for the child. Not only that, but it seems that many other things besides physical pain are harmful. For example, we think that it's wrong to harm someone emotionally or psychologically. For example, sexual abuse does not always result in physical harm, but it often causes grave emotional and psychological harm. We also think that we do harm to someone by denying them an education, by separating them from their family or friends, and so forth. And what about the harm we do to animals or the environment? Should the good or bad use of freedom be determined only by the harm we do or don't do to other persons? Besides this, there is the question: since we are social creatures, is it really possible to harm only ourselves without harming others?

So there seems to be some truth in the position that a source of moral standards is that we should do no harm, so long as it is understood broadly to mean do no harm to others or myself. For harming someone means taking away the good which is necessary or useful for a thing's perfection or happiness. And if this is what we mean by "harm," it is clear that it is bad to harm others or ourselves and good not to harm others or ourselves. So from these considerations, we can formulate a general moral principle: do not harm yourself or others by taking away the goods necessary or important for happiness. And if a choice involves some harm either way, then choose the one which causes the lesser harm.

That's already a good start on moral standards. But we seem to have overlooked another important question: is the moral standard "do no harm" sufficient? It seems that it overlooks another half of our moral experience, in fact, the more important half of moral experience. This other ingredient to our moral life is that we should also seek to do good for ourselves and others, not just avoid evil.[1]

---

1   In fact, St. Thomas Aquinas holds that it is more important to do good than to avoid evil, thus even when some evil might happen through our failure, we should still take risks to strive for those difficult goods. For example, a young man might fear failure in marriage, but the good of marriage is so great that he should not let his fear discourage him from striving to achieve this great good.

If each person looks honestly into their heart, they realize that they can't simply find happiness or fulfillment in avoiding harm. We also find within ourselves the basic need to strive for good for ourselves and others. It is not enough not to harm ourselves, we ought also to strive to attain the goods which are most of all conducive to happiness: peace, truth, wisdom, friendship. And we don't just want these in their bare minimum forms so that we can function. Rather, we want these in their most excellent forms (what traditional morality calls "virtue."). Our desire for goodness also extends to others, so that we see a kind of moral obligation to strive for the good of ourselves and others. So now we can formulate a more complete moral principle: "Do not harm yourself or others by taking away the goods necessary or important for happiness; and strive for an abundance of the goods necessary and important for happiness for yourself and others." But then the next question which naturally arises is: What is good for ourselves and for others?

WHAT IS GOOD FOR A THING MUST BE CONNECTED TO ITS NATURE

At first, it might seem that what is good for a thing is completely relative. Sometimes opposite characteristics seem to be good for something or somebody. Ferocity is good for a dog guarding the house against a robber, but bad for a dog playing with a child. Heat is good in an oven but bad in a refrigerator. Constancy is good when opposing injustice, but bad when justifying bad behavior. Being two-footed is good for a man but bad for a cow.

So is there some definite rule by which we can tell what is good or bad for something or someone? St. Thomas Aquinas offers this insight:

> For it is manifest that the proper perfection of all things is not the same, but different for different things, whether we take the diversity which is between different species, as between a horse and a cow, whose perfections are diverse, or between a genus and the species, as between animal and man; for something can pertain

> to the perfection of man which does not pertain to the
> perfection of animal. And so sometimes it is necessary
> to consider the good of animal and the good of man, or
> of horse and of cow; and the same must be said about
> the bad. For it is manifest that "not to have a hand" in
> man is bad, but not in a horse or in a cow, or even in
> an animal as an animal; and one must speak similarly
> about good and bad in actions.[2]

So the general rule is that to determine what is good for something you have to know what kind of thing it is: what its nature is.
In other words, *what is good for a thing is relative, but not to customs
or laws or desires, but rather relative to its nature.*

WHAT DOES "NATURE" MEAN?

At this point, you may be wondering: "What on earth does he
mean by 'nature?'" You may understand quite well what it means
to say that you went to the countryside "to be out in nature," or that
"she doesn't dye her hair: that is its natural color." But all this talk
about "human nature" sounds very foreign.

The way in which I am using the word "nature" is not unrelated
to those more ordinary uses of the word. What you find in the countryside is what grows up on its own, if man does not take pains to
alter it. The natural color of someone's hair is the color it would have
if not artificially dyed. So in this sense, the natural is the opposite of
the artificial. A natural thing spontaneously comes to be on its own.
It is not shaped or put together from the outside like an artificial
thing. All living things, including human beings are of this kind.
They do not need to be put together like a chair or a house. They
are born, and grow into some definite thing on their own, and their
development seems to arise spontaneously from within them. If I
show you a block of wood and ask you: "What is that supposed to
be?" you would likely answer, "Whatever you want to make of it:
a statue, a pipe, whatever." Artificial things aren't supposed to be

2 *Disputed Questions on Evil*, q.2, a.4, c.

anything on their own: someone else forces them into some shape or design. But on the other hand, if I were to show you an orange seed or a small puppy, and asked you: "What is it supposed to be?" you would right away answer: "An orange tree" or "a dog." So when I talk about nature, I mean "what a thing is supposed to be or become on its own." And this is something very familiar to everyone. It is not some special experience reserved for philosophers. The reason we can tell the difference between healthy babies and deformed babies is because we know what they are supposed to be. Everyone notices when a baby is deformed, not just philosophers. So the way in which I am using the word nature is not so foreign after all.

In order to answer distinctly questions about something's nature, we typically use definitions. For example, if you were to ask me: "What is the nature of animal?" I could say in a vague way: "It is what an animal is supposed to be or become." But that answer is too general. What you really want to know is: distinctly what is an animal supposed to be. And the answer to this question would be the definition of animal. An animal is a living being capable of sensation. Similarly, if you ask me: "What is bird nature?" I could say: an animal with wings and feathers. And if you asked me: "What is human nature?" I could say: man is an animal capable of reason. That is what any human being is supposed to be or become.[3]

The nature of a thing is also the source of its proper movements or actions. As the song goes: "Fish gotta swim and birds gotta fly..." Fish swim because of what they are, birds fly because of what they are. However, in material things, there is always the possibility of some defect. For example, a bird born with one wing still has a nature which is supposed to be able to fly. The fact that we think there is something wrong with a one-winged bird is a clear sign that we know that something with bird nature ought to have two wings.

---

3   Notice that not anything that can be defined has a nature. I can give definitions of artificial things too, but since they are not supposed to be something based upon their own internal principles, but are only intended to be something by an artisan who forms them from the outside, artificial things are not properly said to have a nature.

Now that I have cleared up what I mean by "nature" we can return to the main point I had made: what is good for a thing is relative to its nature. What is good, then, means what helps it to become what it is supposed to be. The good is perfective of a thing, what preserves, promotes, or completes or harmonizes with it in some way. But obviously what completes a thing depends entirely on what that thing is, on its innate tendencies, on what it by nature is striving to be or should be. Eyes help to complete a horse, but are superfluous to an oak tree or a stone. Knowledge of Geometry helps to form or complete the human mind, but is irrelevant to a squirrel. Conversely, whatever prevents the perfection of a thing's nature is bad for it. Not having eyes is bad for a horse, not knowing truth is bad for the human mind.

THE GOOD OF A THING IS ITS PROPER ACTIVITY

Given that what is good for a thing is tied to its nature, can we discover more precisely what kinds of actions would be good for a thing of a given nature? In fact, experience shows that when something has a proper activity, that is, *the activity which it alone can do or which it does best*, this activity is also the good or purpose for that thing. When we ask about what is the good of something, we are implicitly asking about its purpose. Often we will simply use the expressions: "what's that good for?" and "what's its purpose?" interchangeably. The good of a thing is not only what it can be used for. Certainly, this is true for a mere tool or instrument. The good of a knife is to cut, and this is a useful good. But the good of a thing can also be its intrinsic perfection. The good of an eye is to see, and seeing is a perfection of the eye itself, not merely its utility.

Finding the purpose of things is sometimes easy and sometimes difficult. If I ask you: "What's the purpose of a knife?" You immediately say: "To cut." If I ask you: "What's the purpose of an ear?" Again, you know right away: "To hear." But as soon as I ask you: "What's the purpose of a man?" You draw a blank. It's difficult to identify the purpose of a man, so we should approach it through something easier to know.

So it turns out that the purpose of a thing is also its proper or distinctive activity. We can manifest this inductively.

What's the purpose of a knife? To cut. What's the proper activity of a knife? To cut. What's the purpose of a shovel? To dig. What's the proper activity of a shovel? To dig. What's the purpose of a pen? To write. What's the proper activity of a pen? To write. And in general we can say that the purpose of any tool is its proper activity.

What's the purpose of an eye? To see. What's the proper activity of an eye? To see. What's the purpose of an ear? To hear. What's the proper activity of an ear? To hear. What's the purpose of a nose? To smell. What's the proper activity of a nose? To smell. And in general we can say that the purpose of any organ is the same as its proper activity.

What's the purpose of a teacher? To teach. What's the proper activity of a teacher? To teach. What's the purpose of a doctor? To heal. What's the proper activity of a doctor? To heal. What's the purpose of an architect? To design buildings. What's the proper activity of an architect? To design buildings. And in general we can say that the purpose of any profession is the same as its proper activity.

What's the purpose of the ability to play basketball? Actually playing basketball. What's the proper activity of the ability to play basketball? Actually playing basketball. What's the purpose of bravery? Brave actions. What's the proper activity of bravery? Brave actions. What's the purpose of free will? To act freely. What's the proper activity of free will? To act freely. And in general we can say that the purpose of any habit or power is the same as its proper activity.

So the purposes of a tool, of a bodily organ, of a profession, of a habit or power are all the same as their proper activities. So in general we can see that the purpose of any thing is the same as its proper activity.

Now let's go back to the purpose of a man. It's not so hard to identify the proper activity of a man, so we can discover man's purpose by identifying man's proper activity. What is the activity which man alone can do, or which he does best? To act according to reason. So man's purpose, his good, is to act according to reason.

But lots of things are proper activities of man, so why is reason special? For example, why isn't building houses, or painting pictures, or composing music man's purpose since all of these are proper to man?

Notice, I didn't say that man's proper activity is to reason, but to act reasonably or according to reason. Man is not just a mind, man is not just the power to reason, he's an animal with reason, so it is proper to man to act with reason, not just to reason. We might add to the examples just given other ones like playing ball with your son, singing a song, or doing geometry. What they all have in common is that they are all examples of acting reasonably. Having reason is the cause of all of them in some way, so that each properly human activity is ultimately reduced back to man's ability to reason. So when we say that man's proper activity is to act reasonably, we do not simply mean that the act of reasoning is the only activity distinctive to man, we also mean that the ability to reason is presupposed to all of the other activities which are distinctly human. So all of those activities in some way are man's purpose. This helps us to see the wide latitude of things which contribute to or constitute human happiness. Man finds happiness in some degree whenever he acts in a reasonable way.

A sign that we have made a true assertion when we say that human beings should follow reason is that if anyone should object: "why should human beings follow reason?" they would be asking for a reason to follow reason. In other words, they would be admitting the very principle that they are questioning. It is self-evident that we should follow reason. And since the nature of man is to be an animal capable of reason, following nature for human beings means following reason.

HOW DO WE FOLLOW REASON?

So far we have established two main truths: 1) What is good and bad for things depends upon their nature; and 2) Since man's nature is to act reasonably, right and wrong in human actions depends upon acting reasonably, namely, following reason. But how does someone follow reason in the concrete, particular choices one makes? To assert that we should "follow reason" or "act reasonably" is too vague to give us any concrete direction in concrete actions. It would be like a doctor telling his patient, eat healthy food and do healthy things. True as it may be, by itself, that's not very helpful.

Here we can bring together the conclusion that we should follow reason with the conclusion that the good of a thing is tied to its nature. Why should we follow reason? Because reason alone is able to understand what things are and their purposes. In other words, reason alone is able to see the natures of things and hence, their purposes, the reason why they exist and what they are good for. We can also understand the order that one thing has to another. I can see, for example, that a pen is for writing and a knife is for cutting. I can see that the study of medicine is ordered to the production of health in a sick person, and so forth. When we look at ourselves and the natural things around us, we also perceive their purposes and order. I know that eyes are for seeing and ears are for hearing; that the stomach and intestines are for digesting, and so forth. We can see that plants are necessary as food for animals, that water and earth are necessary as food for plants and other living things.

This order we perceive in the natural world is so remarkable that the best human minds over the centuries have only begun to scratch the surface of all the remarkable order contained in nature. For example, just a couple hundred years ago, most scientists thought that cells, the basic building blocks of living things, were mostly simple, jell-like blocks, without much complexity. But now we know that even the simplest cells have a complexity comparable to an entire city. Whether or not someone thinks that this order is the result of an intelligent and wise designer of nature like God, the fact is indisputable that the order is there, however it got there. And even the most brilliant human minds put together could not design even a simple living organism, much less the whole order found in nature.

So not only do we perceive the purposes and order of things with our reason, but we also appreciate the goodness and beauty we find there. The proper response to this is to love this profound natural order, and to respect the purposes of the natural things we know, especially the purposes of our human bodies and abilities. So following reason not only means "using things well" but it also means to act in such a way that respects the purposes of natural things and to love the natural goods brought about when those things are used according to their purposes. This is most of all important when interacting with other persons. It is worse to abuse a human being than to abuse a squirrel.

We can summarize our explanation of good human actions by saying that acting well is to act in a way that most of all fulfills the purpose of human life and respects the purposes of other persons (and even the natural things around us). And the purpose of human life is fulfilled especially in knowing and loving other persons. So good human action is not indifferent to what we are as human beings: it is not just the ability to act however we want, nor is it merely something negative, to act in a way so that we do *not* hurt ourselves and others. It is something positive that perfects what we are and the natural order around us.

OBJECTIONS AND ANSWERS

Objection 1: All this talk about "natures" is so abstract, and seems to be something only philosophers talk about. No one can be certain whether abstractions like "nature" even exist, so we can't make "natures" the basis of our choices and actions.

Answer: The word nature may be unfamiliar, but the thing it refers to in human experience is so familiar and concrete that it is the basis of the great majority of our actions. The natures of things are so familiar in fact that, like the air we breathe, we tend to overlook them. Whether you like it or not, you are constantly making concrete judgments about things based on what they are. If you treat your son differently than your dog, you are admitting that they are different kinds of things. If you treat your dog differently than your salad, you are making that judgment based upon what a dog is and what lettuce is. That's all "nature" means here: "what something is supposed to be." There is nothing at all abstract about natures other than the fact that the name might be unfamiliar. So to say that you are uncertain about whether "abstractions like natures" exist is equivalent to saying that you are uncertain whether your son, your dog, and your salad are different kinds of things and should be treated differently. But it is exceedingly obvious that these things are different kinds of things. In other words, it is exceedingly obvious to everyone, not just philosophers, that different natures exist.

Objection 2: There are no such things as stable natures. Evolution proves that natures are always changing. So marriage and family must change as well.

Answer: This objection assumes the truth of a particular theory of Darwinian evolution. But since it is easier to refute this position by simply granting the premise than arguing against it, let us assume this theory of evolution is true for the sake of argument.[4] As already pointed out, the theory of evolution does not posit that the nature of this or that individual is not stable. Evolution is supposed to work through the mechanism of reproduction, and so it does not refer to a change of nature in an individual, but rather it refers to the offspring having a different nature from the parent. Moreover, evolution is supposed to work so gradually that the change from one generation to another is imperceptible. So even if one were to grant the premise that natures somehow change from one generation to another, this would not account for the sudden, radical and universal changes which are asserted about marriage and family. If the proponents of the new definitions of marriage and family pretend to base their new definitions on the premise that human nature is changing, it would mean that all or most human parents suddenly gave birth to a new species, and that most children are different species from their parents. A frivolous assertion that has no foundation in reality or experience and, therefore, does not deserve a serious reply.[5]

The falsehood of the premise that human nature has changed can be manifested in another way. Remember that by the term "nature"

---

4   I do think that a materialist form of evolution like that posited by Darwin (and Empedocles many centuries before him) can be refuted, though perhaps some form of non-materialist evolution could be justified.

5   Many of the more thoughtful proponents of so-called "homosexual rights" realize that in order to justify homosexual activities they must make such frivolous assertions. They have used popular media, especially movies and television directed towards children as a vehicle of propaganda in order to introduce the false position that human nature is constantly radically changing into something else. For example, the X-men movie series, Ratatouille, and Zootopia all include this assertion. Unable to make an actual argument, they fall back upon science fiction and fantasy to sway the minds of children to adopt these false and harmful positions.

I mean what a thing is supposed to be or become. So what is man? Man is an animal with reason. That is human nature. First of all this means that he shares the natural inclinations common to all animals: the natural desires to eat and drink and breathe and reproduce (recall the distinction made above between natural desires and conscious desires[6]). Of these natural inclinations, the inclination to reproduce is the most fundamental, belonging to all living things, not just to animals. (In fact, the entire theory of evolution mentioned above is based upon the fact that living things are inclined to successfully reproduce. The one thing that evolution in principle cannot eliminate is the natural inclination to reproduce!). Moreover, no one thinks that human beings will move past the desire to eat or breathe. All the more so human nature cannot move past the natural inclination to reproduce. Same-sex unions involving sexual love therefore cannot be justified by an appeal to human nature. They are contrary to human nature in the most fundamental way possible. As regards the rational aspect of human nature, children continue to be the same kind of things their parents are: capable of knowing what things are, their purposes, and the order among them. Human children still require an education, still benefit from having both a father and a mother, and still benefit from living in a lifelong communion. None of the elements of human nature from which we argued to the definitions of marriage and family have changed over the past 30 years (or past 3,000 years!). So that must mean that our natures are stable after all.

Objection 3: Modern science has established that human beings, like other living organisms are really just complicated machines. Therefore, the only difference between us and other things is the physical arrangement of our atoms and molecules: we are all fundamentally the same nature.

Answer: Any account or explanation of our moral experience has to explain that experience, not explain it away or offer some replacement for it. If the objector here is trying to establish that there is no

---

6 Chapter 1, answer to objection 10.

significant difference between human beings and dogs and salads, and therefore we can treat them however we like, this is simply ignoring what is most certain about our moral experiences, our sense of right and wrong. And such an account of right and wrong would make the atrocities of Nazi Germany seem mild in comparison. It is certain that the one who makes this objection believes that he should be treated with more respect than a salad. Salads, after all, do not make objections or offer reasons for their positions. So even if one were to hold the position that there are merely mechanical differences between human beings and other living organisms, these differences would have to be treated as making essential differences in the way we act. So to this degree, we don't need to answer the question about what makes human nature different from dog nature. That there is a significant difference is evident enough.

A word ought to be said, however, against the position that living organisms are merely complicated machines. There is no need to appeal to modern science to establish the claim that living organisms are made up of non-homogenous parts which often function like the parts of a machine. This is evident enough to the senses: the fact that there are smaller parts still comes as no surprise. Yet for all this, our own interior experience of our life and unity manifest that there is a radical difference between us and a machine. The parts of a machine are distinct individual substances, and so the whole machine is really a multitude of many interacting individuals, and not truly a single individual thing that is acting. In contrast, we are aware that we are, simply speaking, a single individual thing, and our parts have a secondary existence. It is more true to say that I see a movie than to say my eyes see a movie. It is more true to say that I wrote the words than that my fingers wrote the words. I experience my parts as me, not as different substances from me. So in living organisms there is a substantial unity that is not present in a machine. And that experience of my unity is more certain than any conclusion I might reach in science. Before I can know a science I have to admit that there is an "I" capable of knowing. So all my knowledge presupposes that I am a single substance capable of knowing. Any so-called scientific theory that concludes to the position that human beings are not individual substances capable of knowledge destroys its own credentials, since it asserts that the scientist himself is not one thing and also that there is nothing which knows.

Objection 4: Modern technology allows us to change our natures. For example, a sex-change operation can make a man into a woman or vice-versa. Therefore, we do not have to follow the nature we happen to be born with if we use technology to change it.

Answer: First of all the example put forward is a false example. Men and women have the same nature: both are rational animals. So a change from one to the other would not constitute a new species or kind of animal. Secondly, a "sex-change" operation is a misnomer. Such surgeries together with hormone treatments only succeed in giving the outward appearance of a change in sex. Every cell in their body still indicates that the individual is one sex or the other. If someone were to clone them, their clone would not take on the any of the characteristics of the opposite sex. A "sex-change" operation does not change their sex any more than a shrub sculpted into an animal shape makes a shrub into an animal. Only the outward features are changed. Larger breasts or facial hair do not make a woman or a man. A woman is someone who naturally ought to have the capacity to bear children. A man is someone who naturally ought to have the capacity to produce semen and beget children.

That being said, the differences between men and women are not insignificant, even if they are not, strictly speaking, a difference in their natures. Male and female are not species-making differences, as some feminists would posit; nor are they mere accidents indifferent to the individual like hair color, as some transgender activists would posit. Rather, they are properties or inseparable accidents or attributes flowing from human nature. Reason can see that human nature ought to have both sexes and that each has a complementary role to play in the propagation and upbringing of our species. Man and woman each have half of the reproductive organs for our species, and consequently play complementary roles in begetting and educating children. Therefore, an individual's desire to have a sex-change operation is unreasonable on two counts. First, such an operation does not in fact change their sex, it simply makes it look that way in a superficial manner to others. Secondly, because sexual differences are for the good of our species, it is contrary to the intention of human nature to reject one's biological sex. This would be similar to the case of someone who wanted to amputate their healthy hands or feet. Nature intends us to use our hands and feet for the good of our species. Amputating them frustrates the good which nature intends. Similarly, destroying our healthy reproductive system does the same.[7]

Objection 5: Gender is really a social construct, and now that we have the technology to change men into women and women into men, people ought to have access to these procedures so that their body conforms to their internal awareness of their own identity.

Answer: Modern activists of so-called "gender theory" attempt to alter language in order to justify their ideologies. They make a false distinction between "gender" and "sex." According to this false distinction, "sex" is biological, while "gender" is a social construct, and refers to the way in which someone inwardly experiences the way they want to manifest their sexuality. For example, a biological male may self-identify as having a female gender, and hence should have a right to change his body to conform to his self-identification.

In reality, when someone self-identifies as something contrary to the objective reality, this is a sign of a psychological illness, not a sign of nature failing to provide the appropriate body. Gender ideologists hold that *whoever wants to transform their body in a way that makes it conform more to their self-identification has a right to do so*. But this principle must apply not only to reproductive organs, but

---

7   The case of hermaphrodites does not contradict this conclusion. Since human nature is partly material, and material things sometimes fail to achieve their end, art can be used to help as much as possible to achieve nature's intention. If someone were born with a deformed hand, art (e.g., some kind of operation) could be used to form something approximating a hand. Similarly, if someone were born with imperfect reproductive organs, art could be employed to approximate a healthy reproductive organ of one sex or the other, depending upon which one could be best approximated.

to all bodily organs (in fact, nearly every organ in the body, from the brain to the bones, differ significantly between men and women, not just the reproductive organs). And so those who self-identify as amputees would have a right to sever healthy limbs. Those who self-identify as a certain race would have a right to modify their skin and facial features to conform to their self-identification. Even those who self-identify as another species of animal would have the right to surgically alter their bodies to conform to this self-identification as much as possible. It is exceedingly clear that the problem with such people is not their bodies, but their mental health. And authentic charity for such people means helping them change their minds, not helping them change their bodies.

To be sure, there are times when surgical intervention to transform someone's body is warranted. Nature does sometimes fail to provide healthy and functioning bodily organs. For example, when someone is born with an obstruction in their digestive tract, removing the obstruction is good. But when someone is born with healthy organs, it is not good to desire to change or mutilate them. And it is not difficult to see the difference between healthy organs and unhealthy ones.

There is another form of collateral damage that takes place when people assert that the differences between men and women are simply social constructs rather than natural differences which are good and healthy. The moral expectations which we have of men in relation to women are destroyed. For example, the moral obligations of men to protect women and to provide for them is destroyed by an ideology that pretends that there are no significant natural differences between men and women.

For example, a man may claim his rights are being infringed because he is subject to being drafted into the military, while women are not subject to this. Assuming that women have no special moral claim to being protected by men, and are in fact equal to men in every way, it would be a very great injustice that he is required to expose himself to death, when women are not. Since risking one's life is a greater harm than changing one's gender, it would seem more just to force women to take hormone supplements, etc., then to force men to risk their lives.

Other absurd conclusions follow as well. Take the following imaginary scenario: two men are at a bar, one of them, unprovoked, starts insulting the other and throws his drink on the other and then starts hitting him. The second man, fights back, and because he is a better fighter than the first man knocks him out in defense. How do we morally evaluate this scenario? We probably say the first man had it coming, and blame the second man little or not at all. But what if the first guy in the scenario were a woman? According to the new gender theories, this makes no significant difference.

Objection 6: Instead of following nature, we should follow what belongs to us as individuals. For in making decisions and choices we should take into account most of all the particular, individual aspects of our lives. Simply making decisions based upon our nature is too generic to make particular decisions in the here and now. Hence when there is a conflict between our human nature and our distinctive traits as individuals, we should follow our individuality, e.g. our inborn inclinations, temperament, etc., since these are more truly our "selves." Therefore, obedience to all kinds of desires fitting the inclinations of the individual would be morally acceptable, even if they happen to be contrary to the inclinations of human nature in general. For example, persons with same-sex attraction should be able to follow this individual trait.

Answer: First of all, it is obvious to everyone that individual inclinations cannot be the sufficient reason for the goodness or badness of someone's choices. Some are born with temperaments or inclinations that are obviously bad to follow, such as a violent temperament or a genetic predisposition to alcoholism. The fact that these inclinations are characteristic of someone as an individual does not make them the standard of moral actions. And how do we judge which individual traits and inclinations are good and which ones are bad? Based upon whether they conform to human nature. Why is a violent temperament bad? Because human beings are naturally social, and violent actions destroy peace in society. Why is the disposition for alcoholism bad? Because man is a rational animal, and alcoholism causes someone to be a slave of a substance that impairs his reason.

And so what makes it good or bad to follow is not that it is one's own, and inborn, but that it either fits with or conflicts with the human nature that is common to us all. Our inclinations are good or bad based upon what we are supposed to be, not based upon how we happen to be when we are born. There is a likeness to this in the matter of health. The standard by which we determine whether an organ is healthy or not is its purpose, which is based on common nature, not on the preferences or unique characteristics of an individual. So if a man is born blind, or without limbs, we do not conclude from this individual trait of his that this is natural to him and good for him.

This does not mean that individual traits are insignificant in each person's pursuit of their good. These individual traits can make a difference in *how* they pursue human goods. For example, someone with a keen intelligence might pursue the virtue of knowledge or wisdom more energetically, while someone who is very empathetic might pursue the virtues of charity and mercy more effectively. Nevertheless, these individual traits do not determine *whether* certain actions or choices are good or bad: wisdom is good and error is bad even for the person of lesser intelligence. Mercy is good and lack of compassion is bad even in the person who is naturally less empathetic. The flexibility in the good for man allows for this difference of emphasis or manner of pursuing virtue, fitting the different temperaments. But whether they are good or bad is still measured by human nature.

Objection 7: Our natural inclinations are sometimes bad. For example, it seems natural for children to fight when they disagree: "boys will be boys." And well before they marry, a young man and woman who fall in love have a desire for sexual intimacy. And nearly everyone has a natural tendency to eat more than is healthy. Therefore, we should not follow our nature.

Answer: This objection once again is due to the confusion between natural desires (better called "natural inclinations") and conscious desires.[8] A natural desire is not a conscious desire which we cannot choose not to have. Instead, a natural desire is an inclination for

---

8 See chapter 1, answer to objection 10.

some action that is perfective of our nature. Many of the so-called "natural" tendencies which are bad are not the tendencies of human nature itself, but of our individual traits or inborn temperaments, and it is not "nature" in this sense that we are supposed to follow, but human nature itself. A good example of this is the genetic predisposition to drink alcohol unreasonably.

It is true that some bad tendencies common to all or nearly all the human race seem to be inborn, and are not just a matter of personal temperament. The examples given in the objection seem to be of this sort. But even the fact that they are common to all human beings does not prevent us from seeing that they are bad. It is possible for a trait to happen to be common to all humans without flowing from human nature. For example, "being in the Milky Way Galaxy" is common to all humans, yet is not demanded by human nature. And it is quite possible in some scenario that every human have brown eyes, yet this is not demanded by human nature. Similarly, it is possible that there be some kind of inherited genetic defect that happens to belong to all humans, but the fact that it belongs to everyone would not prevent us from seeing that it is a defect since it impedes the good operation of human nature. If most humans died leaving only those with the inherited genetic defect of blindness, so that all future children were born blind, we would be no less certain that blindness is bad than we are now, since human nature demands the ability to see for its full perfection. The inclinations to over-eat, to fight in children and to unreasonable uses of the reproductive power in teenagers are examples of this sort. They are practically universal, yet also can be seen to be incompatible with human nature. They seem to be a kind of inheritable corruption of human nature itself and of its tendencies. The Christian faith teaches that the cause of this corruption is Original Sin (which G.K. Chesterton called the one dogma of the faith for which there is adequate empirical evidence). But we do not need Christian revelation to see that these things are bad.

In summary, we can say: "Follow nature" does not mean "Do what comes easily and effortlessly," but "Act according to the intrinsic purposes of your natural abilities, in keeping with their relative importance."

Objection 8: We should not, indeed we cannot, follow nature, since nature often conflicts with itself, inclining us to contrary things. For example, men naturally seek pleasure and avoid pain, but we also have a natural desire to do what is reasonable. But sometimes these conflict, as when doing the reasonable thing is painful. It is natural to desire food, and also to desire the well-being of our child, but if there is only enough food for one of us, these natural desires conflict. Again, we naturally desire to do good and avoid evil, but sometimes doing good necessarily involves doing evil, as when for the sake of the good of saving our life, we choose the evil of having a gangrenous limb amputated.

Answer: Sometimes things are thought to be naturally good when considered in the abstract, that is, when prescinding from particular circumstances and the judgment of reason, but when considered in their circumstances and by the judgment of reason they take on the aspect of evil. For example, maintaining one's bodily integrity is naturally good considered abstractly by itself, but if one adds the circumstance that a limb is diseased and will cause death to the whole body, then keeping this limb takes on the aspect of evil, and amputating it is not contrary to reason, but good. And so while one good may be contrary to another in the abstract, a particular reasonable good never conflicts with another reasonable good in such a way that we are forced to choose something truly evil. The question is: how does reason judge among goods and evils in such a way to determine what is the reasonable good in these particular circumstances? I will address this question more fully in the next chapter in which I will provide some tools for determining which choice is reasonable when goods seem to conflict.

Objection 9: Often we act contrary to the natural purposes of things and it is clearly not wrong. For example, we can spay a dog or a cat, drink diet soda, wear earplugs, etc. All of these seem to be examples of acting contrary to nature and yet none seems to be wrong. Therefore, acting contrary to nature is not the cause of evil in human action.

Answer: This objection is really a series of related objections, each of which needs its own proper response. As for spaying a dog or a cat, such examples misunderstand what is meant by the expression "follow nature." Following nature does not mean follow the nature of each natural thing, and never frustrate their natures. Instead, it means follow *human nature*. It would be natural for a lion to want to eat me, but is it wrong for me to frustrate that lion's natural desire? Of course not! Because he possesses reason, man can use plants and irrational animals for his own purposes, and sometimes it would be harmful to human nature to allow pets like dogs or cats to reproduce within a given environment. So it is perfectly reasonable and natural for a man to spay a dog or a cat in some circumstances.

This being said, one should not conclude from this that human beings should only be concerned about themselves with complete disregard for the natures of other things. Human nature does not exist in isolation from other natures. To the contrary, human nature has a very definite relationship with other natures. Of all living beings, man alone has the capacity to perceive the whole good of nature, that is, the right order among particular natures. For example, only man can see that if all water is taken away, this will destroy all living things since all living things depend upon water for nutrition. Even in more particular cases man can see the right order which should exist among natures. Many decades ago, cattle were imported to Australia where they had never existed before. After a short time, a large percentage of grazing land was covered with dung, and grazing land was fast becoming rarer. Since no cattle had existed in Australia, neither did dung beetles which serve to process cattle dung so that it fertilizes the soil instead of harming it. So dung beetles were also imported and the natural balance of the ecology was restored. So man has a certain responsibility as a steward to the whole natural order. Nevertheless, it is natural for man to put other natures to his use even if this means frustrating their particular ends so as to order them to more universal ends. For example, by eating a salad, man frustrates the natural inclination of lettuce to live and reproduce, yet he orders this lettuce to a higher end, namely the preservation of his own existence. We will take up the question of a hierarchy of ends in nature in the next chapter.

In response to the objection about diet soda, using some ability contrary to its purpose, just for the sake of pleasure, or for some other motive, is always unreasonable, and hence is wrong to some degree. But sometimes there is such a small disorder involved that little or no fault is attributed to the person who acts that way. For example, it is always wrong to steal, but to steal a paperclip from a rich man does so little harm that it is not considered harmful at all. Something like this happens with diet soda. If someone drinks diet soda solely for the pleasure but not at all for its nutritional value, this is a minor form of gluttony. But since it does little or no harm to the individual or others, it is not considered a serious defect. And if there is some annexed reasonable good to such things, this may itself remove all fault. For example, simply the good of hydration would be enough to justify the reasonableness of drinking diet soda, and the good of avoiding cavities enough to justify chewing sugarless gum. There probably would be a moral fault however if someone exclusively drank diet soda.

In response to the case of wearing earplugs, people usually wear earplugs to prevent loud noises from damaging their hearing, or to prevent distractions. It is not natural to listen to noises so loud that they would damage hearing. Moreover, there is nothing unnatural in temporarily impeding hearing provided it is not at a time when someone ought to be hearing. For example, if hearing noises would prevent needed sleep or distract from the use of a more noble ability, such as study, then it is perfectly natural to impede hearing under such circumstances. In short, one is still following nature, because one is preserving the natural power, or ordering it to other things that are naturally more necessary or better. In other words, within man himself there is a hierarchy of abilities, and there are times when it is reasonable to temporarily disable one ability for the sake of something better. It may even be necessary to temporarily disable some natural ability for the sake of preserving that very ability, as sleep is necessary to preserve the good use of reason.

Objection 10: It is not always true that we should follow reason. Often the best thing to do is trust our heart or go with our instincts.

Answer: This objection misrepresents what is meant by "following reason" and also leaves the meaning of "trusting our heart" and "going with our instincts" ambiguous.

First of all, following reason does not mean ignoring past experiences and memories or our good habits in favor of a logical calculation about what should or should not be done. Nor does it mean following the conclusion of any kind of argument whether it is certain or not. Rather, it means that whatever choices we make should be choices for which we have a good reason. Sometimes the best reason we can give for some action is the guess we make based upon past experiences and choices or the character of persons involved, etc. For example, in judging whether or not we should trust someone's opinion, we might not be able to give a proof that his opinion should be believed, but we can make a probable guess that he is to be trusted in this case based upon the fact that he has been kind and honest with us in the past. Now if this kind of probable evidence based upon past experience or memories is what is being called "trusting our heart" or "going with our instincts," then following our reason is not opposed to "trusting our hearts" or "going with our instincts." It is simply one way of following reason when that's the best evidence we have.

On the other hand, if "trusting our heart" or "going with our instincts" means following our emotions when there is no evidence whatsoever that these emotions correspond to reality, then following reason is opposed to "trusting our heart" or "going with our instincts." Whatever choices we make must be based upon some reason, even if the best reason we can give is merely probable.

Notice too that when someone does have a certain proof of some truth, then there is not the slightest question about following reason. No one "trusts their heart" or "goes with their instincts" when a conclusive reason can be given which contradicts the inclinations of our heart or instincts. Your heart might incline you to trust someone who says that the sum of the inner angles of a triangle is less than two right angles (180 degrees), but once you have seen the proof that this is impossible, you will follow reason instead. Whenever reason provides a certain proof, it is clear that reason must be followed.

3
Choosing Between Conflicting Goods and Evils

MANY OF THE DIFFICULTIES WHICH AROSE IN
the previous chapter about nature and reason as sources of moral
standards concerned the potential for conflict among goods and
evils, especially the case where it seems that our choices or actions
necessarily involve some kind of evil. In order to resolve these apparent conflicts it is first necessary to set down some principles of order
by which someone can judge which goods are to be preferred to others, and which evils can be permitted for the sake of certain goods.

THE HIERARCHY OF GOODS

If every good were equal to every other good, and goods were
mutually exclusive so that sometimes in order to follow nature we
would have to act contrary to our nature, then we would be in a bind.
But if some goods are better than others, and some natural inclinations are more natural than others, then we can still follow nature
by pursuing the goods which are more perfective of our nature and
by following the inclinations which are more essential to human
nature. And, in fact, it is the case that some natural inclinations are
naturally subordinate to others. For example, the inclination to care
for one part of our body, such as our hand, is subordinate to the
inclination to care for a more important part of our body, such as
our head. That is why we will instinctively allow our hand to take a
blow in order to protect our head. An analogy from human affairs
can help here: The precept "obey legitimate authority" is a valid
precept even if the command of a lower authority conflicts with the
command of a higher authority. Insofar as a lower authority contradicts a higher authority, it ceases to have authority, and so need not

be obeyed. For example, if we are supposed to obey a sergeant, but the captain over that sergeant gives us a contradictory command, we know right away that we should obey the captain, since the sergeant bears authority only from that captain. The same principle can be applied to natural inclinations and desires. If a natural inclination which is supposed to be subordinate to a higher natural inclination resists the higher inclination, it ceases to be natural. For example, emotions are supposed to be subject to reason. Therefore, if your emotions resisted the judgment of reason, then the inclinations of your emotions would cease to be a natural inclination. And, therefore, following nature would mean resisting your emotions and following reason. The same principle applies wherever a conflict arises between a lower and a higher natural desire. So the next thing that we need to determine is which natural inclinations are higher and which are lower.

HIERARCHY OUTSIDE HUMAN NATURE

If we consider natures other than human nature, we discern among them a certain order or hierarchy. Non-living things like soil and water seem to exist as nourishment for the sake of living things like plants. Among living things too there is an order: animals are better than plants, having the same basic abilities to take in nutrition, grow and reproduce, but including also the power of sensation which is better than anything a plant can do. Plants also seem to be for the sake of animals, since nearly all animals use vegetable matter for nutrition. Finally, man is over all other animals: man has sensation like other animals, but adds reason above this. Man also makes use of other animals, not only for nutrition, but even for higher ends, such as work. And finally, man not only uses other natures, living and non-living, but he also perceives the order among these natures and is perfected in knowing this order. It is good for a human being to know the reasons for other things and their mutual relationships. Man is the pinnacle of nature precisely because in man alone can the whole of nature somehow be brought together: summed up and united in human knowledge.

HIERARCHY WITHIN HUMAN NATURE

Within human nature too we discern an order and hierarchy. Man, like a plant, has the ability to take in nutrition, grow and reproduce. But like animals, man has sensation. And finally, man has the ability to reason. Not only are these abilities clearly distinct from one another, but they also have an order proportional to the order found outside human nature. It is better to sense than to take in nutrition or grow. No sane person would choose to lose all his senses for the sake of gaining the longevity of a tree. And among the senses themselves, there is an order. Given the choice between the senses of taste or smell and the senses of hearing or sight, it is obvious that hearing and sight are preferable. And better than sight or hearing is reason. It is obvious that it is better to lose your eyesight than to lose your mind. Even in reason itself, there is a kind of order. For example, knowledge about practical matters (what is to be made or done) is inferior to knowledge about truth for its own sake, which culminates in wisdom. A sign of this is that practical knowledge is always for the sake of something better than itself, while the knowledge of truth for its own sake is good in itself.[1]

Human persons are naturally members of families because certain goods which perfect human nature would be impossible for an individual human person. A newborn infant left to itself would die in a short time without a family. Even a mature adult left to himself would be helpless to begin his own family. Begetting and raising children requires cooperation between spouses. This is not only true as regards provision of physical necessities, but also the education of

---

1 Joseph Pieper sums this up well in *The Purpose of Politics*: "All practical activity, from the practice of the ethical virtues to gaining a means of livelihood, serves something other than itself. And this other thing is not practical activity. It is having what is sought after, while we rest content in the results of our active efforts. Precisely that is the meaning of the old adage that the *vita activa* is fulfilled in the *vita contemplativa*. To be sure, the active life contains a felicity of its own; it lies, says Thomas, in the practice of prudence, in the perfect art of the conduct of life. But the ultimate repose cannot be found in this kind of felicity. *Vita activa est dispositio ad vitam contemplativam*; the ultimate meaning of the active life is to make possible the happiness of contemplation." From *Joseph Pieper: An Anthology* (San Francisco: Ignatius Press, 1989), p.121.

the mind and will require parental guidance and discipline. And so it is natural for man to seek and prefer the common good of family life over the merely private goods afforded by a solitary individual life. For example, all things being equal, it is better for persons to live together and take meals together within their families than for each one to choose where he prefers to live, or what he prefers to eat at a given time. The sacrifice of individual freedoms is worthwhile for the sake of living in closer communion with family members.

But since the human family is not sufficient to provide the goods which most of all perfect human life, man is also naturally part of a larger society, what the ancient Greeks called the *polis* and the ancient Romans called the *civitas*. Such a political society can be defined as one which is capable of bringing human nature to its full, natural perfection. No family, for example, is capable of perfecting human nature in the arts and sciences. A family left to itself is at most capable of providing basic food, shelter and moral formation. It requires political society on the order of what is found in a city to realize the highest abilities of which the human person is capable. This is most of all clear in centers of higher education which aim at inculcating wisdom; but any number of arts and sciences such as sculpture, painting, architecture, mathematics, ethics, etc., are only possible in the context of civil society. And so the common good of the city or state, of which man is also naturally a member, exceeds even the common goods of family life. This is why, for example, a young man is expected to leave behind his family in order to defend his country.

Finally, beyond the common good of political society is the common good of our species. No national interest, no matter how compelling, ought to be preferred to the good of our human race. For example, a devastating nuclear war which would kill most humans on the planet could never be justified by appeal to patriotism to one's country.

So looking back at this hierarchy of goods, we find that the good of human nature excels the goods of other natures (e.g., men are better than cabbage and dogs). The goods which perfect the better parts of human nature are preferable to the goods which perfect the lesser parts of human nature (e.g., an education which perfects the mind is better than a pair of glasses which perfect the eye-sight). Finally, the common goods of the family and civil society are preferable to the private goods which perfect only an individual (e.g., national prosperity is better than wealth for a single citizen, and peace in a family is better than one person always getting their way). Appreciating this hierarchy of goods within and outside of human nature makes it possible to choose between apparently conflicting goods and natural inclinations in such a way that one is always able to follow nature and follow reason.

HOW TO KNOW WHAT TO CHOOSE WHEN GOODS CONFLICT

Now that we see that there is an order among reasonable goods, and the objects of our natural desires, the next step is to determine some principles by which the good which most of all fulfills our nature can be chosen in particular circumstances. The following are some tools which will assist one to choose the reasonable good when goods seem to conflict. These are not the only tools which might be necessary, but they are some of the principal ones.

COMMON GOOD SHOULD BE PREFERRED TO PRIVATE GOOD

The first principle for choosing a reasonable good is to *choose your common good over your private good*. A word should be said here about what is meant by the expression "common good." Both the words "common" and "good" have many meanings in the English language. Putting the two together multiplies the possible meanings this expression could have. Here I have two principal meanings of "common good" in mind. The first meaning is what I would call a common good in the perfect sense, namely, a good which is able to be shared by many at the same time without being diminished. For example, the definition of marriage, or the Pythagorean Theorem are common goods of this sort. They can be understood by many at the same time without in any way being diminished. Peace within a family or country are common goods in this sense: the individuals who experience this peace do not cut off some part of it and leave the remainder with the others. God is a common good in this sense: he can be known and loved by many at the same time without being diminished.

In a secondary or imperfect sense, the common good can be defined as a good which is able to be shared by many, but either 1) not at the same time, or 2) at the same time but not without diminishing. A common reservoir of water can be shared by many at the same time, but not without being diminished. The part of the highway I am using right now can be shared by many cars, but not at the same time. In contrast to both of these kinds of common goods are private goods: goods which, for whatever reason, cannot be shared by many.

When I set down the principle that someone should prefer his common good to his private good, I mean especially the common good in the perfect sense. A common good in this sense is not merely the sum or aggregate of private goods. For example, the common good of national prosperity does not simply refer to the sum total of wealth of each individual in a nation. National prosperity refers to something that can be shared and enjoyed simultaneously by each member of the society without being diminished. Similarly, national peace is not merely the sum total of individuals who are not fighting in a nation. It refers to the quiet that follows from right order among all the citizens within that country. Peace in a nation (or a family) can simultaneously be enjoyed by all the members without being diminished. And the truth possessed as a common good of many persons is not merely the sum total of knowledge of each individual. If it were, then if one individual died, the truth held by all in common would be diminished. But the selfsame, undivided truth exists wholly and completely in each individual, so that it is neither diminished when it is shared, nor is it depleted when one who possesses it ceases to be.

It is obvious to human experience that the common good should be preferred to the private good, and this is based upon the fact that the common good is a greater good for the individual than his private good. A man or woman knows that it is better for them to sacrifice their private good of being free to do what they want on

their own, in order to live together in a loving family where everyone lives and does things together. Again, it is better for people to
sometimes make public promises which they are expected to keep
so that the members of that society can share in common the good
of a sense of security that they will be able to count on one another.
For example, it is good for people to promise to remain in a marriage
and that society expects this of them even if it means great personal
sacrifice at times so that the greater good of stable families can exist.
A musician knows that it is better to conform himself to the notes of
a given piece and playing style of the conductor and orchestra than
to play his own notes in his own style, otherwise there could be no
beautiful orchestral music. A citizen knows that it is better to live
under laws which sometimes restrict individual freedoms for the
sake of living in a community where common action leads to the
possibility of human perfection. Even nature teaches the preferability
of the common good over the private good: the hand instinctively
sacrifices itself to defend the head from a blow, and animals sacrifice
their own lives to protect their young.

One further possible misunderstanding should be cleared up here:
the common good is not merely the good of an impersonal group of
individuals without being the good of the members of that group.
Such a good would be an alien good, not properly one's own good.
This would be akin to the communist notion of common good, the
good of a whole machine in which each part is merely a tool to the
good of the whole, but does not truly enjoy this good as their proper
good. A common good is truly *your* good, not merely someone else's
good. When a number of students together learn some truth, the
truth is not possessed by "the class" as if it didn't belong to any of
the individual students, but only to the whole class. In fact, in such a
case it only belongs to the class in virtue of belonging to each of the
students.[2] So a truly common good is not opposed to one's proper

2   Sometimes it is true that the common good more properly belongs to
the whole than to any individual member. For example, victory belongs more
properly to the team than to any one member of the team. Yet each and every
member of the team is truly victorious: victory belongs to each of them as
their good too.

good, rather it is opposed to one's private good.[3] Indeed, the common good is more truly your own good, than your merely private good, and furthermore it is your greater good. Otherwise it would not be reasonable to prefer your common good to your private good.

For the sake of further clarifying this distinction, it will be helpful to offer some additional examples where the distinction between the common good and the private good comes into consideration.

Example 1: A basketball player chooses between playing so as to achieve better individual statistics (e.g., a higher scoring average) or playing so as to increase his team's chance of victory (e.g., by letting more efficient players on the team handle the ball more often). Since the good of victory is a common good, it should be preferred to the private good of better individual statistics.

Example 2: A man chooses between saving his own life and sacrificing his life for the lives of his family or country. Since the good of the family or country is a common good, it should be preferred to the private good of one's own life.

Example 3: Someone chooses to amputate a diseased limb. Because the good of the whole body is better than the good of the limb, then it is good to choose to amputate the limb for the sake of preserving the life of the whole body. But if the disease could be stopped without amputation, one should choose that.

Example 4: A man who knows he is innocent of a crime but is reasonably judged to be guilty in a public forum must choose

---

3   The "proper good" and the "private good" are similar in many ways, and since similarity is often a cause of confusion, people often confuse a "proper good" with a "private good." Both are goods that can belong to an individual person. Yet a "private good" belongs *only* to one person, and is incapable of belonging to anyone else at the same time. In contrast, a "proper good" can belong fully to multiple persons at the same time. Some examples may be helpful to manifest the difference between "proper good" and "private good." A child is the proper good of its parents, but is not the private good of either one: for the child belongs to both parents, not only to one. Peace in a society is a good belonging to each person in that society, so it is a proper good of each person in that society. But it is not a private good of any of them, since it does not belong exclusively to one of them. Truth is the proper good of someone who knows that truth. Yet it is not their private good, since it can easily belong to others too.

between accepting the punishment and resisting the punishment. Since abiding by just laws is a common good (even if they are erroneously applied) while his own freedom from punishment is a private good, he should choose to undergo the punishment. This is what Socrates chose for the sake of the common good. Arguing against his friend who is trying to persuade Socrates to escape an unjust death sentence, Socrates says:

> If the laws and the community of the city came to us when we were about to run away from here, or whatever it should be called, and standing over us were to ask: "Tell me, Socrates, what are you intending to do? By attempting this deed aren't you planning to do nothing other than to destroy us, the laws, and the civic community, as much as you can? Or does it seem possible to you that any city where the verdicts reached have no force but are made powerless and corrupted by private citizens could continue to exist and not be in ruins?"[4]

If someone decides that his own judgment about his guilt (rather than a public verdict) is to be the determining factor about how he should act or be disciplined, then he must hold this is true for all in the society. Thus, whoever disagrees with a public verdict can do as he wants, and laws will only bind those who agree with them. But very few if any will agree with being punished. Such a disposition toward law, that each man is the judge of their application, would certainly destroy the society.

PRIVATE GOOD OF A HIGHER NATURE SHOULD BE PREFERRED TO PRIVATE GOOD OF A LOWER NATURE

The second principle for choosing a reasonable good is to *choose the private good of a higher nature over the private good of a lower nature*. A simple example will suffice here. When choosing between the life of a dog and the life of a man, one should choose to save the

---

4   *Crito*, 50a-b.

life of a man because a man has a higher nature than a dog. Sometimes it is not clear which thing has a higher nature. Should you save
your cat or your dog? Such cases do not invalidate the principle,
since the reason why it is difficult to decide is not because the principle is false, but rather because it is difficult to see if either one has
a higher nature. If it were clear, the decision would be relatively easy.

THE GOOD-IN-ITSELF SHOULD BE PREFERRED TO WHAT HAPPENS TO BE CONNECTED TO A GOOD

The third principle for choosing a reasonable good is to *choose
what is good-in-itself instead of what happens to be connected to
something good.* This distinction[5] may seem difficult at first, but it
is a distinction we constantly use in our moral reasoning, as some
examples will help illustrate. If I study well and learn a subject, then
I will be able to pass an examination. But I can also pass an examination by looking at the answers of a person next to me and copying
his answers. Learning a subject is good-in-itself, and through that
very knowledge I am able to pass an exam. But copying another
only happens to be connected with passing the exam (in fact, if the
person I copy has not learned the subject, I will not pass the exam).
Or to take another example, a prison warden may agree to release a
woman's innocent brother on the condition that she fornicate with
him. But the release of her brother only happens to be connected
with her act of fornication. Fornication is not in itself ordered to the
release of the innocent. The warden may even decide not to release
her brother afterwards.

These are clear enough examples, though sometimes the examples
are more difficult. Should I lie to a Nazi who asks me if I am hiding
Jews? Here again, the same principle is at work. In itself, lying does
not save the Jews I am hiding in my house. What may end up saving
them is the decision of the Nazi not to search my house, and he may
decide this whether I lie or not. In fact, if he believes me when I say

---

5   In traditional philosophical terminology this distinction is referred to as
the distinction between the *per se* and the *per accidens*, Latin phrases meaning
"through itself" and "through what happens."

something it is only because he trusts that I am not a liar. In itself, lying destroys the very basis for this trust. This does not mean that I am obliged to tell the Nazi that I am hiding Jews, but there are other ways of accomplishing the same result of convincing him not to search my house without actually telling a lie.

Additional examples will help to illustrate this distinction.

Example 1: If someone promises to feed my starving children on the condition that I kidnap someone else's child, then I should choose not to kidnap the child. For kidnapping the child would not be the true cause of my children being saved. Rather, the will of the person who has the means to feed my children is the cause, and he may or may not feed my children if I kidnap someone else's child.

Example 2: If someone is dying so that vital organs (say the kidneys) have ceased to function, and has a choice to use a machine to replace the function of his vital organs, then he is not morally bound to use such a machine, especially if it places an extraordinary burden upon the person. For the cause of death, in itself, would be organ failure. It only happens that this can be forestalled temporarily by a machine.

So ultimately, choosing what happens to be connected to a good means choosing something that, in itself, has no reason to be connected to that good, which is another way of saying that there is not a reason for choosing it, but only what seems to be a reason. Therefore, someone who chooses what only happens to be connected to some good is not following reason. In any case, it is good to be aware of this distinction to avoid faulty moral reasoning. But sometimes it can be very difficult. Plato once said that this distinction is so difficult to see that it sometimes deceives even the wise.

THE PRINCIPLE OF DOUBLE EFFECT.

It sometimes happens that some human acts involve an unavoidable evil, yet it is clear that they ought to be done nonetheless. This is not a case of the object, end or circumstances of the act being evil in themselves. If that were true, the whole act would be bad. Rather, this is a case of an evil which is foreseen as an *effect* of the act, but is not intended as *part* of the act. To determine whether or not one should choose to do an act where there is a foreseen evil, the principle of double effect[6] must be applied. The conditions of the principle of double effect are as follows:

1) A good must be intended.

2) The foreseen evil must not be intended either as a means or as an end.

3) The good intended cannot be caused by the evil.

4) The good intended must outweigh or at least be of equal weight as the foreseen evil.

5) If multiple means can equally accomplish the good, then the one with the least foreseen evil should be chosen.

These conditions ensure that the object, circumstances and end are all good. Conditions 1) and 2) must be present for the end or intention to be good. Condition 3) must be present for the object to be good. And conditions 4) and 5) must be present for the circumstances to be good.[7]

Let's take some examples to help clarify. A pregnant woman has a cancerous uterus which cannot be treated without killing the baby, and which will certainly result in the woman's death if it is not treated. If she has the uterus removed is that a morally good choice?

Is there a good intended? Yes, the saving of her life. Is the foreseen evil intended as a means or as an end? No. She does not intend the death of her baby as an end. Indeed she wills the opposite. Nor is the death of the baby willed as a means. The means she intends here is the removal of the cancerous uterus which happens to result in the death of the baby. Is the evil the cause of the good? No, since the death of the baby in no way causes her improvement of health, rather it is the removal of the cancerous uterus which causes her restoration to health. Is the good of greater or equal weight as the

6   This principle of moral decision making is called "double effect" since it is foreseen that the act will have both a good and an evil effect.

7   This is a reference to the fact that for any choice to be good three elements, the object, the end intended, and the circumstances must *all* be good. A developed treatment of this doctrine is beyond the scope of this book, but if the reader wishes to understand this doctrine better, a good book to read is: *Ethica Thomistica: The Moral Philosophy of Thomas Aquinas*, by Ralph McInerny (CUA Press) 1997.

foreseen evil? Yes, since each life is taken to be of equal value. More-over, if it is certain that the baby would have died anyway, it is better that only the baby die than that both the mother and baby die. So overall, this can be a morally good choice. If there is a good chance that the baby could live if the uterus is not removed right away, then it would also be a good choice for the mother to sacrifice her own life so that her baby could live. Indeed it would be a better choice, though either choice would be morally acceptable.

On the other hand if a woman were to have an abortion in which the life of the baby was directly taken, this would not be a good choice. For then the evil would be the cause of the good, and the evil would be intended as a means to the good. So both the intention and object would be evil in such a scenario. Therefore, a direct abortion is always morally wrong, since it always involves intentionally taking an innocent life.

Another example will help to illustrate the principles. Suppose a man or woman chooses to undergo chemotherapy even though it is foreseen that this will result in infertility. There is a good intended: saving his life. Is the foreseen evil the cause of the intended good? No, infertility does not cause health. Is the foreseen evil willed as a means to the intended good? No, since being infertile is not willed as a means to destroy cancer. Is the good of greater or equal weight as the foreseen evil? Yes, since saving one's life is better than saving one's fertility. Indeed if one lost his life he would also lose his fertility. So, overall, this is a morally good choice.

OBJECTIONS AND ANSWERS

Objection 1: It is self-centered to say that human nature is better than other natures. Every species is equal in dignity, and it is merely because of our tendency to preserve our own species first (probably as a result of evolution) that we act like we are a superior species. Therefore, there is no hierarchy in nature.

Answer: This objection is an example of the fallacy of positing the wrong cause. The argument which I gave for the hierarchy of natures had nothing to do with how humans feel about other species, or the fact that we are inclined to preserve our own species over another species. Those were never premises in the argument. Instead the argument focused upon two obvious facts: First, higher species have what the lower species have, and then add something more (for example, animals can grow and reproduce like plants, but then they add above this the ability to sense). The second obvious fact is that the higher species have objectively better abilities (for example, it is obviously better to reason than to see with our eyes: for who would rather lose their mind than their sight, even if he had the sight of an eagle?). To these two obvious facts, we can add another reason why one species is superior to another, namely that the lower are for the sake of the higher. Eating and nutrition is clearly for the sake of conscious life in animals and in man. We do not live for the sake of eating, we eat for the sake of living. So that means that the ability to take in food is ultimately for the sake of something better. Similarly, the ability to sense is for the sake of reason. A sign of this is that we judge our sense powers to be healthy when they contribute best to providing matter for our mind. For example, not hearing well often causes a learning impediment.[8] As to the objection that this argument is self-centered, we are even aware of a superiority of non-human species over other non-human species. That isn't the result of evolution making us want to preserve our own species.

---

8   A fourth reason can be given for the superiority of one species over another: by knowledge the perfections of other things can be present in the knower. For example, the color which is a perfection of the apple, can somehow be present in the one who sees it. So obviously one who knows is better than one who does not, since the knower possesses its own perfections, as well as the perfections of other things, while the non-knower, like a plant, only has its own perfections. Of the senses, the sense of touch seems to be the least extensive, only taking in the perfections of things with which it comes in direct contact. But sight is better than touch precisely because sight most of all seems to extend farther and take in more perfections of things. Finally, intellectual knowledge seems to be the most extensive of all, taking in the perfections of beings of every kind. Therefore, the higher the mode of knowing the more perfect the knower must be.

Objection 2: Sometimes the private good is better than the common good. For example, my act of contemplating God, or my act of loving my spouse, which is a good belonging to me alone, is better than winning a basketball game, which is a good I share in common with my teammates.

Answer: When I say that one must prefer his common good to his private good, I mean when these goods fall within the same order. For example, some goods are merely physical or sensible or emotional, like winning a basketball game, or moving a heavy object with a group. Other goods are spiritual, like the knowledge or worship of God, or knowledge and love of some other person. Because a spiritual good is a good which utterly transcends physical goods it happens that a private good of the spiritual order is better than a common good of the physical order. But if that same private good of the spiritual order be compared to a common good of its own order, for example if my private act of worshiping God be compared to the act of worshipping God in common, then the common good still has primacy. So it can happen that a certain private good is a greater good than some common good, but this is never true of it *because it is private*. Indeed the fact that it is private is a sign that it cannot be the best good since its goodness is completely exhausted by one individual, whereas a common good is not exhausted by one individual, but is so good that it can be shared by many without being diminished. And so if some private good is better than some common good it is despite the fact that it is private, and because it belongs to a higher order of goods.

Objection 3: Sometimes it is better to pursue private goods. For example, it is sometimes better for a husband or wife to go out with friends and leave the rest of the family home. Or sometimes it is better for the sitting President of the United States to go on a vacation than to work all the time.

Answer: In regard to the first example, friendship is not a purely private good. It is also a kind of common good which is close to the common good of family life. Even so, choosing to be away from one's family for the sake of being with one's friend would be reasonable only in the case where the family does not depend on the presence of that member for a significant good during the time he will be away. For example, the common good of the family does not require that the father be present at all times, but only at the times where his contribution is essential or important (e.g., in supporting his wife, in disciplining the children, or directing the affairs of the household). It would be the same in other cases where it is reasonable to choose a private good for a time, namely, this would be reasonable only when choosing this private good does not come into conflict with securing the common good. Thus, it is reasonable for the President to go on vacation, so long as there are not urgent matters of State to attend to. Moreover, the primary reason why the vacation is good is because it assists him in being able to return to his duties with renewed attention and energy.

4

Right and Wrong in Matters Pertaining to the Family

NOW THAT WE HAVE SET DOWN THE PRINCIPLES of moral standards, and given some tools for solving moral dilemmas, we are in a better position to judge whether the various views given above about the family and marriage are good or bad. The definition of family we proposed above was the communion between a husband, his wife and their children. The definition of marriage we proposed above was the lifelong communion between a man and woman, established by their free consent, for the sake of the generation and education of children. We can now manifest that any understandings of marriage or family contrary to these are wrong.

SEXUAL ACTS WHICH CANNOT BE ORDERED TO PROCREATION ARE WRONG

Sexual acts which cannot be ordered, in themselves, to procreation are wrong because they do not follow nature or reason. Often it is asserted that the only requirement for a sexual act with another to be good is that it is done from love, or at least does not hurt anyone. But the question which must be asked is: are all sexual loves good or not?

Clearly some sexual love is good, since it is necessary for the continuance of our species, and the continuance of our species is good. But clearly some sexual love is bad (for example, adultery, polygamy, incest, necrophilia, pedophilia, bestiality, etc.). Therefore, it is not enough to assert that two people love each other sexually to justify this as a moral good. The facile argument so often used today to support applying the name "marriage" to legal contracts between persons of the same sex is easily refuted in this way. "How would you like it if you could not marry the person you love?" is the question often posed. The answer is: some loves are wrong, very wrong, and in no way justify marriage.

How then can a judgment be made between right sexual love and wrong sexual love? Let's first look at a more universal question: When have we used anything rightly or wrongly? What is the difference between right use and abuse? In anything that can be used, it has an intrinsic purpose: a pen is intrinsically for writing. To use it to write is a right use. To use it to dig is an abuse. So using something according to its intrinsic purpose is good, while using something in a way that is inconsistent with its intrinsic purpose is an abuse. So to answer the question about the right use of sexual love, we need to see what the intrinsic purpose of sexual love is. Right sexual love fulfills the intrinsic purpose of sexual love, while wrong sexual love is inconsistent with and does not fulfill the purpose of sexual love. Since reason can determine the natural purposes of the reproductive organs, following nature and reason means using the reproductive organs in a way consistent with their natural purpose.

There are two basic positions that someone could take about the intrinsic purpose of sexual love: 1) that sexual love is for the sake of generating children; or 2) that sexual love is for the sake of physical pleasure and emotional satisfaction. Which of these is the true purpose of sexual love? We can show that generating children is the purpose of sexual love in many ways. First of all, the purpose of a thing is not just anything it can do, but the best thing it can do. Children are obviously better than pleasure and emotional satisfaction. Ask any parent which they think is better, their child or the brief pleasure they experienced in conceiving the child? Second, pleasure is found in the exercise of many bodily functions: it is not proper to sex. Pleasure is the bait that nature uses to get people to fulfill the purposes of their natural abilities. For example, nutrition is better than the pleasure in eating, but nature uses the pleasure of eating as bait to get us to eat. The pleasure associated with natural activities is obviously for the sake of getting us to perform those natural activities. So the natural activities must be the ultimate purpose rather than the pleasure. Third, the purpose of a thing should explain its structure. For example, since the purpose of a knife is to cut, it must have a blade which is hard and sharp. But pleasure does not explain what happens in a sexual act. On the other hand, generating children does explain this: Why do the reproductive organs behave the way they do when a person feels sexual love? Because it maximizes the chances that a sperm will be united to an egg in a place where a new life can grow and develop. Finally, if the purpose of sex were simply the brief experience of intense pleasure and nothing more, it is hard to explain why there are such profound psychological, emotional and physical effects associated with sex. The proponents of a free-love, laissez faire view of sex seem to have difficulty explaining why sex is no big deal, while simultaneously holding that it is impossible to live without. In contrast, the intrinsic connection between sex and the continuance of our species explains why sexual activity has such profound effects. If the very purpose of sex is the continuance of our species, and is so profoundly rooted in our nature that reproduction is common to all living things, this explains why nature has ensured that both the positive effects of sex ordered to procreation and the negative effects of sex not ordered to procreation are so significant.

From the fact that uses of the reproductive organs which cannot be ordered to procreation are wrong, it follows that the state should in no way endorse them. For they cannot in themselves contribute to the common good, and they will certainly result in grave harm to the society which tolerates them, and even graver harm to the society which positively accepts them.

OBJECTIONS AND ANSWERS

Objection 1: The purpose of sexual love is neither pleasure nor begetting children, but rather the communion of persons: it is clear that sexual love brings persons closer together, so any sexual expression ordered to love and communion is good.

Answer: The intrinsic purpose of a thing must explain its organization and structure. But as is the case with pleasure, the communion of persons does not explain the order or structure of sexual activity (namely, why it is intrinsically linked to making procreation possible), hence it cannot be its purpose. Moreover, many kinds of communion have no relation to sex at all (for example, the communion between parents and their children), and many sexual acts have no relation to communion (for example, masturbation). This would not be true if the primary and intrinsic purpose of sexual activity were communion.

Recall that a communion is a sharing of life between persons. But sharing sexual pleasure or emotional satisfaction together is not a sharing of life proper to persons. It is rather a kind of common enjoyment proper to animals. This is not to say that the communion between a husband and his wife cannot be enhanced by sexual intimacy. In fact, the very fact that a sexual act is ordered to procreating a child makes that act a kind of beginning of a shared life, since the child is the common good of both spouses, and presupposes that they intend to share a life together raising their children. So it is principally through the generation of children that sexual activity can promote the most profound communion between a man and woman.

Objection 2: For many people the purpose of sexual love is pleasure, so to use sexual love for pleasure is not wrong.

Answer: As noted earlier in the answer to objection 4, in chapter 1, it is important to distinguish between the motive why someone does something, and the intrinsic purpose of a thing. The motive is the extrinsic purpose someone gives to a thing. While the intrinsic purpose of a thing is based on what the thing is good for in itself. For example, the intrinsic purpose of studying medicine is to acquire the ability to heal, but the motive why some particular person studies medicine might be to make money or even to kill. The intrinsic purpose of a thing is the basis used to determine whether or not it is being used well or abused. A sign of this is that the motive someone has is judged right or wrong based upon the intrinsic purpose of a thing.

Finally, if pleasure were the intrinsic purpose of sexual love, then any sexual act which resulted in pleasure would be enough to justify the goodness of the pleasure experienced through that sexual love. But masturbation, adultery, polygamy, incest, necrophilia, pedophilia, and bestiality all result in pleasure for the person acting out of sexual love for these things. Clearly, taking pleasure in these things is wrong in the extreme. But if we hold to the principle that the generation of children is the purpose which justifies sexual love and makes it right, then all these forms of sexual love can be shown to be wrong: masturbation, necrophilia, pedophilia and bestiality all involve sexual love in which there is no natural ability for reproduction. The others (incest, polygamy, adultery and fornication) all involve doing something which is ordered to generating children in circumstances which are harmful to their upbringing and well-being. For example, in the case of polygamy, the education of the children and peace within the family is greatly harmed because of a multiplicity of wives and the fact that jealousy easily arises among wives and children. And in the case of incest, incompatible family relationships will be mixed together (e.g., the wife will also be a child of her husband: which is incompatible since wives should be treated as equals to their husbands, but a daughter should not be treated as equal to her father).

Objection 3: Something could have two purposes. For example, the mouth can be used both for eating and speaking. In the same way, reproductive organs can be used both for procreation and pleasure.

Answer: Pleasure is associated with the use of nearly every bodily organ, though especially with those most necessary for preserving the individual and species, namely eating and reproducing. So pleasure is not the proper purpose of any bodily organ. Secondly, there is a clear order between sexual pleasure and reproduction, just as there is a clear order between the pleasure of eating and nutrition. Pleasure is for the sake of inclining animals (not just man) to perform those acts which are good for the species and for the individual. And since the good of the species is greater than the good of the individual, nature equips the reproductive act with a more intense physical pleasure than eating. So these pleasures are for the sake of nutrition and reproduction. No one could reasonably claim that nutrition was for the sake of pleasure or that their children were for the sake of pleasure. Moreover, if someone used their nutritive power exclusively or even habitually for the sake of the pleasure it produced (e.g., always drinking diet sodas, or eating so long as pleasure was involved) it would obviously harm one's health. Similarly, using the reproductive organs exclusively or habitually for pleasure harms man's social bonds (for example, the divorce rate in marriages which habitually use contraceptive is many times higher than those which do not), and if most people did this, our species would die out.

As for organs that serve a dual purpose in man, like the mouth, we can see that some of the structures of the mouth, lips, tongue and throat are such that they are well suited for both functions.[1] On the other hand, other structures serve only one purpose of the other: for example, the vocal chords contribute to speaking, but not to eating, while the taste buds contribute to eating, but not to speaking. So the mouth is actually a complex network of organs, not a single organ. Eating is more necessary than speaking, but speaking is better than eating. And in contrast to the reproductive organs, the dual purposes of the mouth are not subordinated one to the other as happens with pleasure and reproduction. Speaking is not for the sake of eating, and eating is not for the sake of speaking. Each one has its own purpose. A sign of this is that both functions cannot be carried out well simultaneously: eating and speaking are mutually exclusive. So both eating and speaking explain, in part, the structure of the human mouth, but both together explain it fully. On the other hand, reproduction alone explains the structure of the reproductive organs, and even explains why they should have the structure to cause such intense pleasure associated with the reproductive act. A sign of this is that pleasure and reproduction happen simultaneously, and the greatest pleasure is typically experienced when the reproductive act is carried out in a way most apt to generate children.

---

1   For example, see Aristotle, *Parts of Animals*, II, c. 16, 659 b 30 –660 a 27.

Objection 4: Many same-sex couples show genuine fidelity and con-cern for one another. These things are clearly signs of a good and reasonable relationship. Therefore, this evidence shows that for some people homosexual relationships are reasonable.

Answer: Fidelity between married persons means using one's power of reproduction exclusively and reasonably with one's spouse. Such "fidelity" would not be a sign of virtue in a same-sex couple because they are using their power of reproduction unreasonably. Similarly, a father who has consensual sex with only one of his daughters could not be praised as "faithful" for such acts. On the other hand, genuine concern for another person is praiseworthy, but such concern has nothing to do with marriage or sex as such: it is appropriate to any friendship. Just because someone does some morally bad things it does not follow that everything he does is morally bad. For example, someone might habitually abuse alcohol, but might also be very generous in donating to the poor. So all the argument shows is that friendship between persons of the same sex should not be prohibited: a rather uncontroversial position. One should not confuse intimate friendship with sexual intimacy.

Objection 5: In cases where the health of one of the spouses could be harmed by the conception of a child or the transmission of a disease it is obvious that following reason means using contraception such as a condom.

Answer: The use of contraception is not the only means reason sees for avoiding the transmission of a disease or avoiding con-ception to preserve the health of the woman. Reason also sees that abstinence from sexual relations will more certainly obtain this good than any form of contraception. Besides, reason also sees that inten-tionally impeding a reproductive act is contrary to reason, so the only way to follow reason in this case would be by abstinence. This is an example of choosing the good in itself instead of what happens to be connected with the good. Contraception only happens to be connected with the good one is seeking: in itself, destroying fertility does not contribute to health. To the contrary, fertility in itself is healthy. Reason may also judge that the conception of a child in such circumstances is still reasonable, since the conception of a new human life is so great a good that it is often worth significant health risks. Our own children are such a great good that they are certainly worth risking our lives over. As to those who hold that it is unreasonable to expect someone to abstain from sexual relations for an extended period, see the response to objection 14 in the Appendix.

Objection 6: It is not wrong for a woman who is undergoing some treatment which makes her infertile (such as chemotherapy) to have relations with her husband. Therefore, it is not wrong to take pills which make her infertile while having relations with her husband.

Answer: This is a good example of the principle of double-effect. If the sickness is serious enough, so that all the conditions are met for the principle of double-effect, a woman can choose a good even though she foresees an evil. But she can never choose the evil in itself as a means or as an end. This would be the case if she directly intends and chooses to render the reproductive act infertile.

Objection 7: Society will not be harmed by accepting that reproductive organs can be used without being ordered to procreation. How could something that happens entirely in private harm society anyway?

Answer: This objection is very close to objection 13 in chapter 1, so I will incorporate much of that answer here for the sake of convenience, and also add a number of other arguments besides.

First of all, even if one were to grant that society would not be harmed, still the individual who deliberately chooses to use his reproductive organs in an unreasonable way will be harmed, and will be impeded from attaining human perfection.[2]

But in fact, society will necessarily be harmed by accepting that reproductive organs can be used without being ordered to procreation. First of all, the objector maintains that the *society is accepting* the position that reproductive organs can be used without being

---

2   For a very insightful article which describes the moral and emotional harm which comes to those who engage in homosexual activity, see Ronald G. Lee, "The Truth about the Homosexual Rights Movement," (Published in *New Oxford Review*: February, 2006).

ordered towards reproduction. That means it is not a private matter but a matter of teaching a whole society about a wrong use of the power of reproduction. So the assumption that it is something merely private is false.

Secondly, even if it were not a matter of society accepting these acts, nevertheless, while disordered acts of this kind may be done in private, the effects of the acts are not always private. This can be clearly shown by many forceful arguments.

First of all, the morality of an act is not only judged based upon whether someone gets hurt, but also upon whether or not the act is perfective of our nature and respects the natural purposes of our abilities. So even if no one got hurt, it would be morally wrong to enjoy sexual pleasure outside of an act which is, in itself, capable of generating new life. And since society is harmed when one of its members is inclined towards vice, society in fact is harmed whenever an individual performs an act which inclines him towards vice.

Abusing the reproductive power inclines people away from the right use of that power. For example, if a young man habitually masturbates or looks at pornography or fornicates, he develops a craving for satisfying himself sexually by those means. In a short time, those desires obtain a kind of mastery over him, and he often cannot resist the urges to follow those desires. One common effect of this abuse of his reproductive power is the delay of marriage, or even failure to marry. One of the powerful incentives to marriage is the natural urge to use the reproductive power with a spouse. If someone thinks it is acceptable to use his reproductive power outside of marriage, this will remove one of the strongest natural incentives to marriage.

Furthermore, if that young man enters into a marriage, those same desires will be there and he will often be unfaithful to his spouse, if not by outright adultery, at least by habitually looking at or thinking about other women. And even if his spouse is not explicitly aware of this, he will act differently toward his wife than if he were being faithful to her. As a result, there is a breakdown of the intimacy and the sense of security and fidelity in the marriage. Families in which this bond of intimacy between husband and wife are compromised or broken are unhealthy and tend to result in unhappy children, or no children at all.

In marriages where spouses choose to use contraception, the intimacy of communion is harmed or destroyed. In the very moment when that intimacy is expressed and signified by marital relations, the spouses choose to render that act unfruitful. A clear indication of this is that one of the terms used to describe contraception is "protection." We need protection from an enemy. So who is the enemy here? Your spouse? Your future children? How can intimate communion coexist with such a disposition towards one another in marital relations? It is not surprising, therefore, that the factor which most highly correlates with divorce is the habitual use of contraception.

Another likely effect of this abuse of the reproductive power is the taking of human life. To act against life in its seminal stages naturally leads to acting against life in its more mature stages. When men and women do not learn to master their sexual desires, but are conditioned to give in to them, children are more often conceived outside of marriage. This is why in every country where contraception has been legalized, both pregnancies outside of marriage and abortion have skyrocketed.

In addition, when someone does not see the purpose of procreation and the need for the natural family as the right context for a reproductive act, they fail to understand the great good involved in cooperating with that natural order. The goodness of the natural family itself becomes obscured. Anyone who is married and is raising children knows how difficult this is. Unless people in a society see clearly the good of the natural family and of children in particular, they will not, on the whole, be willing to make the great sacrifices necessary to form stable families and raise children. As a consequence, divorce proliferates and the population begins to decrease beyond sustainable levels. Eventually, a whole nation or people dies out. So society at large is harmed by the mindset that accepts separating sexual pleasure from procreation.

This becomes especially evident when society begins to accept that homosexual acts are morally acceptable, and that a union of persons based upon such acts is equal to a natural family. First of all such same-sex unions claim the right to have children (which they can only get by taking them from natural families). These children are raised without a father or a mother: that is a grave injustice to those children when it is done intentionally. The natural consequence of this is the position that every member of a family is expendable and unnecessary: if two moms can do just as good a job as a mother and father, then society is saying that the father is useless and expendable. If two dads can do just as good a job as a father and a mother, then the mother is expendable and useless. This is very harmful to family life.

Furthermore, the natural family is something that precedes the state: natural families existed long before any civil societies did. Same-sex "marriages" are created by the state, and can only continue to exist if constantly supported by the state. When same-sex unions are called by the name "marriage" and are made equal in law to natural marriage the state begins to treat natural marriage and family as if they were the property and creation of the state too.

Furthermore, if the purpose of such unions is to enjoy sexual pleasure together, then why should they be limited to two people? And why couldn't members of the same family, like a father and a son get "married" since they are as capable of enjoying sexual pleasure as any other two people? With natural marriage it is clear that things like polygamy and incest harm the education of the children, so they would be excluded. But there seems to be no reason to exclude such things according to the new definition of marriage. After all, if marriage is utterly unrelated to procreation and raising children what reasonable limits could one place upon the kinds of relationships that could constitute such a "marriage"? Someone might object that the enjoyment of sexual relations is not important for same-sex unions, but if that is the case, then practically any friendship could be called marriage: marriage is not just friendship.

These and many other arguments show that the acceptance in a society of sexual acts which cannot be ordered to reproduction greatly harms that society. Sexual acts are never merely private acts.

WRONG DEFINITIONS OF MARRIAGE BASED UPON THE ABUSE OF THE REPRODUCTIVE ACT

As I pointed out above, all agree that marriage, as distinct from mere friendship, pertains to romantic or sexual love. No reasonable person thinks that two friends or a brother and sister raising children together is a marriage. But in order to follow nature and reason, sexual love must be ordered to reproduction. Therefore, any view of marriage which excludes the possibility of an act in itself ordered to procreation between spouses is a false and wrong understanding of marriage. Thus, marriage cannot be: 1) between persons of the same sex; or 2) between persons who cannot perform a procreative act (for example, because one spouse is missing reproductive organs); or 3) between persons who intend throughout their whole marriage to frustrate the natural purposes of the reproductive act through contraception. Infertile couples are not excluded from marriage, however, so long as they are capable of performing an act which is, in itself, ordered to procreation. The fact that they are infertile does not mean they are not following nature, but rather that nature, having been followed, is somehow disabled in their case.

An objection to this is that natural family planning (NFP) where couples intentionally make use of the periodic infertility of the woman is considered moral by nearly everyone. But to this I would reply that in NFP the structure of the reproductive act remains the same, and no positive impediment is placed in the way of procreation. *In itself* such an act is capable of generating new life, but it doesn't because of something outside the act.[3] It just happens that the couple is temporarily and naturally infertile at the time they engage in intercourse. A couple may use this lawfully if they have good reasons–so long as they have or at the very least intend to have children. For it can be for the good of the children they already have

---

3   In the case of a breastfeeding wife, she is only indirectly responsible for her infertility. She is obviously following nature in providing nourishment for her child, and if the "evil" of infertility happens as a result of this, this is clearly a case of the principle of double effect. Indeed, the fact that breastfeeding typically causes temporary infertility is a sign that nature intends periodic infertility during the first year or so after birth of a child.

that they not conceive now, and that they prove their fidelity to each other through sexual intercourse.

As a consequence of these truths, it is wrong for the state to treat same-sex unions as if they were the same or in any way analogous to marriage. As mentioned above in the answer to objection 11 in chapter 1, while there are some similarities between these same-sex unions and marriage, their differences are so great that they do not even fall under the same genus of definition, much less the same species.[4] The genus of marriage is communion, which as we have shown is a natural union that is perfective of human persons and of human society. On the other hand, the genus of same-sex unions is contract, a legal bond which is not only not natural, but is against nature and reason, and is, therefore, harmful to human society. The fact that homosexual rights activists were still trying to require that same-sex unions be defined under law as equal to marriage despite the fact that all or nearly all the legal rights associated with marriage in many states already existed is a sign that what was really desired were not the legal rights but rather the name "marriage." By associating the name of something which is natural and good with homosexual acts, the intention is to deceive people in to believing that homosexual acts are also good. The equivocation is intended to deceive in order to influence people's thoughts and actions: "which is to be master, that is all."

REPRODUCTIVE ACTS IN CIRCUMSTANCES IMPEDING CHILDREN'S MORAL FORMATION ARE WRONG

It is not enough that someone use their reproductive organs in a way that is, in itself, ordered to reproduction for that use to be good. Following nature and reason also requires that children be generated within a context which provides for their well-being, not just their existence. Following human nature means acting reasonably,

---

4   The terms "genus" and "species" are technical logical terms that refer to the parts of a definition. The genus is the broad part of the definition, while the species is the narrow part. For example, in the definition of man, "rational animal," animal is the broad part, and rational specifies animal to the particular animal which is man.

including reproducing reasonably. And since human children require a father and a mother for their care and moral formation, it is unreasonable to beget children in a context in which this is impossible.

There are many ways in which the moral formation of children might be significantly impeded. First of all, if the union between the parents is not life-long, the children will be denied the stability necessary for proper moral formation. Thus, fornication does not follow reason or nature. Moreover, a union which the spouses consider temporary or conditional so that divorce is seen as a possible choice is not the proper context in which to perform a reproductive act.

Secondly, a disordered relationship between parents could also make the proper moral formation of children impossible. As a consequence, incest, polygamy and polyandry are all unreasonable. Incest results in incompatible relationships among family members. For example, spouses should be equal, but parents and children unequal. Siblings should be able to live in peace in the same home in such a way that the relationship between two siblings is not exclusive of the others, but sexual relationships are necessarily exclusive, etc. And many other disorders enter into a family when immediate family members engage in reproductive acts with one another. In such a case, true communion, sharing of a life together is rendered impossible. Polygamy and polyandry also seriously compromise the moral formation of the children. Rivalries and jealousies inevitably arise among spouses. Children from different parents find themselves unequal to their half-siblings. The potential for more children than can be provided for in polygamy is much greater. And in the case of polyandry, there is no natural way of knowing which children belong to which father. Once again, the possibility for true communion is destroyed in such cases.

The relationship between the parents can also be disordered because of hatred for each other or a deliberate lack of love and concern for one another. The moral formation of children in such cases is clearly impeded. Persons who have no intention of loving one another or caring for one another ought not to engage in reproductive acts, even if they are outwardly in a stable bond. Thus, for example, if persons get legally married for merely utilitarian reasons such as immigration, they should not engage in reproductive acts. Nor should spouses who have chosen not to love one another engage in reproductive acts. For example, a man should not force himself upon his wife against her free will.

WRONG DEFINITIONS OF MARRIAGE BASED UPON THE IMPOSSIBILITY OF MORAL FORMATION OF CHILDREN

It follows from the preceding considerations that any right definition of marriage requires that it guarantee an environment conducive to proper moral formation of children. Conversely, any definition of marriage which implies that conjugal intercourse can take place in a context which makes the proper moral formation of children impossible is a wrong definition of marriage.

Thus, marriage must be between only two persons, one man and one woman, neither of whom can be in the same immediate family as the other. Marriage must also be lifelong. And marriage must be entered into by free consent in such a way that the spouses intend to love one another throughout their marriage. This last condition is implied in the expression "communion . . . established by free consent" found in my original definition of marriage.

From all these considerations, it follows that the only correct understanding of marriage is a lifelong communion of one man and one woman, established by their free consent, for the sake of the generation and education of children.

OBJECTIONS AND ANSWERS

Objection 1: Poor parents cannot provide an education for their children, therefore it would seem that poor people cannot marry or have children, which is clearly false.

Answer: The education referred to here is not primarily academic, but rather moral. Wealthy parents might be in a better position to provide excellent tutors and schools for their children, but they are not in a better position to be an example of moral virtue to their children. Indeed, by modeling fortitude, hope and cheerful love during very difficult financial times, poor parents often have an opportunity to provide an example of moral virtues rarely practiced by the wealthy. However, if the parents are so destitute that they could not even provide for the basic necessities of life for their children, such as food and shelter, then it is true that it would normally be imprudent in such cases to beget children. However, poverty is not by its nature a permanent condition, and so if there were some hope of relieving such extreme poverty begetting children in such hope would even be virtuous.

Objection 2: Many children from homes where their parents are divorced receive excellent educations. Therefore, a lifelong union between the parents is not essential to fulfill this purpose of marriage.

Answer: Again, education as found in the definition of marriage does not primarily refer to an academic education, but rather to moral formation. And for children to see an example of infidelity or inconstancy in love between their parents is clearly not an example of moral virtue. For example, children whose parents are divorced marry at a lower rate, and have a much higher rate of divorce if they marry, than children whose parents are not divorced. In a society like ours where divorce and remarriage are very common, attempts are made to make it seem as if the effects of divorce are minimal. Anyone who has encountered a child whose parents are going through a divorce sees such platitudes as self-evidently false. The truth is that there is not one child who wishes that they did not have a father and mother who love each other. Even from the perspective of the academic aspect of education, it is well known that, other factors being equal, children whose parents have divorced do far worse than children whose parents remain together. And if it sometimes happens that a child does receive an excellent moral formation even though his parents are divorced, experience shows that this is rare, certainly not common enough to justify permitting divorce as a society. Moreover, their good moral formation is not because their parents divorced, but in spite of it. Almost always in such cases, the reason the child was formed well was due to his close contact with a family in which the parents loved each other. And so even the exception only serves to prove the rule.

Objection 3: Soldiers who are going off to war are allowed to marry even though there is a reasonable chance that their children will be fatherless. Also persons with terminal illnesses are permitted to marry even though they know they will not live long enough to provide for or educate any children which may come. Therefore, for the same reason it is not necessary that two persons be committed to a lifelong union when they marry.

Answer: The case of those who do not intend to remain faithful for a lifetime differs radically from those who do, but foresee that they will have a short life together. In the former case, they are themselves the cause of the dissolution of the union, while in the latter case they are not the cause, but rather some other factor beyond their control: war, illness, etc. As a consequence of this, those who intend to remain faithful until death still give a witness to their children of lifelong fidelity (albeit over a short life). Moreover, giving one's life for their country would offer an example of virtue and contribute to the moral education of the child. But being unfaithful to one's spouse would not contribute to the good moral education of the child. So the case of a soldier going off to war or a terminally ill person getting married would be a case of the principle of double-effect: the good of having a child is chosen even though there is the foreseen evil that a parent will not live long enough to educate that child. But in the case of those who do not intend to remain faithful, the evil of separation is directly willed by one or both of the spouses. Moreover, divorce is the result of the spouses choosing to live separate lives, so that their wills are no longer in agreement. This is morally a completely different case than the case where both spouses foresee that one will die soon and still agree to have a child. In the latter case, their wills are united and the spouse left behind to care for the children does not feel abandoned or betrayed; but rather supported by the love of the other and their common decision to bring a child into the world under those circumstances. Thus, the children are never exposed to a family situation where the parents have chosen not to love one another or share a life together. The truth is that divorce is much worse for a child than the death of a parent, since after the death of his parent, a child still has the security of knowing that his parents loved one another. However, it is true that it is morally obligatory in such a case that, if they decide to have a child, the parents make provision for some kind of substitute for the spouse who is likely to die soon (e.g., with a grandfather or an uncle who can guide the children in place of the father, etc.).

Objection 4: After the children are raised and the couple are no longer fertile, there is no compelling reason why they ought to remain together. Therefore, stability while the children are living in the home is sufficient for marriage, and lifelong stability is not necessary.

Answer: The education of children is a lifetime endeavor. Parents give an example of moral virtue and fidelity to one another at every stage of life, so that their children can witness how they ought to behave at the next stage of their own lives. Parents teach their children how to live well after the children are grown, how to live well while experiencing the burdens of old age, etc. Parents even teach their children how to die well. And it is no example of virtue to stop loving someone you have lived with and shared children with for most of your life. Even in ordinary friendship it is obvious that friends ought to stay friends throughout their lives. Besides, spouses should love one another more than their children, and parents do not stop loving their children once they are grown and no longer depend upon them. All the more so should spouses continue to love one another. Finally, communion, which is the genus of marriage, means sharing a life. And no one wants to live only part of their own life. Neither does anyone who lives in true communion with another want to live and share only part of the other person's life.

Objection 5: In some polygamist households there is sufficient wealth to care for all the children. Therefore, so long as the wives are content with the arrangement and they enter into it by their free consent, there is no reason why they cannot marry.

Answer: While material goods are the most necessary for raising a child they are not the most important goods. Much more important are the love, presence, fidelity and moral example of the parents.

Wealth is not a sufficient good to justify having children. A parent might be wealthy enough to pay someone to do everything in raising and caring for their children. But someone who raises children for pay will not provide a child with the upbringing they need; and if the parents themselves are not present to the children and loving the children, their moral formation will be gravely harmed. Nor is it enough that all the parents in a polygamist household are in agreement about the arrangement. A father and daughter might be in agreement about an incestuous relationship too. The objectively disordered nature of the relationship itself harms the upbringing of the children. When a child sees that his father only loves his mother with half his heart, the child too experiences being loved only half-heartedly by his father. Moreover, in such a case, there will be increased fear and insecurity of being abandoned in favor of the father's "other family."

Objection 6: If a person with young children can remarry after their spouse has died, this implies that it is reasonable for children to be raised by parents other than their biological parents, and that the inequality between half-siblings is not an impediment to proper moral formation. Therefore, for the same reason, polygamist marriages and divorce and remarriage are acceptable.

Answer: Even in such cases where the parent remarries after the death of a spouse, there are usually significant differences between the ways the half-siblings are raised. The natural bonds of love which motivate a parent to care for their own children are a great assistance; and often the children which are from the prior union are not treated equally. It is an exceptional person who can care for someone else's child with the same love and care as their own child. Moreover, there is a radical difference between providing a substitute parent for small children due to death of one of their parents, and intentionally choosing your children to be raised by someone other than their biological parent. It is one thing to help a child after it has been hurt and quite another to intentionally hurt them. The same thing can be said about adopted children: it is one thing to give children to someone other than their biological parents because circumstances left no other choice. It is quite another to simply choose to prefer adoptive parents over biological parents, even though the biological parents are capable of raising their own children.

ANY DEFINITION OF FAMILY NOT BASED UPON THE RIGHT DEFINITION OF MARRIAGE IS WRONG

At the beginning of this book I defined family as the communion of a husband, his wife, and their children.[5] It is easy enough to see that at the heart of this definition of family is the definition of marriage. The definition of family is like the definition of marriage fully realized: marriage is a communion for the sake of generating children, family is the communion established once the children have come. What the one is in power or ability, the other is in actual realization. And so the communion of marriage is not some completely different communion than that which existed between the spouses before children come. It is the same communion extended and realized.

From this it is clear that any definition of family which is based upon a false definition of marriage is a false definition of family. Family is not essentially a legal communion (though it may be recognized by law), but a natural and moral communion. Even in the case of adopted children who are not naturally begotten by the parents, still by adoption they enter into the communion of the parents which is something natural and moral.

In the case of a polygamist relationship, even though the children are naturally begotten, it is more true to say that they belong to two families than to say that they constitute one family. A polygamist union does not have the union necessary for a true communion, and so cannot be called marriage. Similarly, the children belonging to the different mothers are not part of the same communion with one another, and so do not constitute one family. The case is similar to a man or woman who is divorced and remarried with children from both unions: the children are members of distinct families (or more properly, at least one set of children do not belong to an intact

5   Cf., CCC 2202.

family at all, but only part of a family, since the parents of some of the children are not truly married).

OBJECTIONS AND ANSWERS

Objection 1: When a couple adopts children, the union of the parents and children is a legal union created by the state. Therefore, at least in the case of adopted children, the family is in part a legal union, not natural.

Answer: The role of the state in adoption is similar to the role of the state in marriage. It is incumbent upon the state to recognize and even regulate marriage for the sake of the common good. Yet this is not the same as causing or creating or even defining marriage. The state must also recognize the rights of persons, who are clearly natural and not created by the state. Nor does the state have an absolute authority over such things as marriage and persons. Rather the state must respect their nature and purpose and ensure that all citizens do the same in their interactions. For example, the state should punish adulterers who break up marriages. Similarly with adoption: the inclination to care for members of our species is natural, not something created by the state. It is natural for adults to care for abandoned children and to raise them in place of their parents. It is also in keeping with the nature of an abandoned child that it be raised by loving adults. So adoption itself is founded upon our nature. The state merely recognizes that adoptions in such cases should take place and regulates them to guarantee justice. So the legal ratification of an adoption by the state is not the cause of the union of adopted children with their parents: it is the recognition that this union has been made in accordance with the demands of nature, and a protection of its security.

Objection 2: The state has the right (and even duty) to take children away from abusive parents. Therefore, the children more truly belong to the state than to the family. Consequently, a family is more properly a legal union than a natural or moral union.

Answer: Here again, the state is not the cause of the dissolution of a family when parents are abusive toward their children. Rather, the state recognizes cases where the parents themselves have compromised the natural communion of the family by grave abuse of the children. The children are not the property of the state, but neither are they the absolute property of their parents. The children are persons who have a dignity from their human nature that must be protected even if the ones who are violating that dignity are the parents themselves. Once again, the inclination to protect innocent members of our species against grave harm is natural, not created by the state. And so it is in response to the natural inclination to preserve and protect our species that children can sometimes even be taken from their parents. So the reason why the state has the power to take children from abusive parents is not because children belong more to the state than to their parents, but because children belong more to our common human nature than to their family. And if the state were not able to intervene, then other persons, such as close relatives, would be obliged to do so. However, the abuse must be very grave, touching upon the basic necessities of life for the state to intervene.

Objection 3: If a wife dies and the father remarries, the new wife and husband form one family with the children from the previous union. For the same reason, in a polygamist household the children can be part of one family with both (or all) the wives of their father.

Answer: In the case of the death of a spouse, the new marriage constitutes a true communion and a true marriage. And therefore, although the children from the previous union are not biological children of the step-mother (or step-father), they can enter into the communion of this marriage in a way analogous to the way adopted children enter into the family of parents who are not their own. But a polygamist household does not form a true communion since it is in the nature of a marital communion that one spouse share their whole life with the other (for no one wants to live only part of their own life). But a polygamist relationship requires that none of the spouses share their whole life.

PART II

The Path of Revelation

PRELIMINARY NOTE
TO PART II

Understanding the Family through Revelation

IN THE FIRST PART OF THIS BOOK, I CONSID- ered the family to the extent that it could be understood and defended from reason alone, unaided by supernatural revelation. In the second part of this book I intend to consider the family from the perspective of what God has revealed about the family. It will be simply assumed for the purposes of this book that Christian revelation is authentic and definitive, and no attempt will be made here to justify this claim.[1] However, since truth harmonizes with truth, it should be expected that what was established in the first part of this book will harmonize with what follows. And this itself will be evidence for the truth of the revelation which supports the conclusions of the second part of this book.

I will consider three primary sources of revelation about the human family: the Trinity, the Incarnation, and the Holy Family. I shall also consider scripture passages which speak about family life. In the third part of this book, I will apply these principles to the Christian family. And since something is easier to understand

---

1 Many excellent defenses of the authenticity and completeness of Chris- tian revelation have been written. For example, the *Summa Contra Gentiles* by St. Thomas Aquinas is the definitive, classical work on this subject. More recent publications include: *Catholic Evidence Training Outlines: A Classic Guide to Understanding & Explaining the Truths of the Catholic Church* by Frank Sheed and Masie Ward; *Handbook of Christian Apologetics* by Peter Kreeft and Ronald K. Tacelli; and *Beginning Apologetics* by Jim Burnham and Fr. Frank Chacon.

when it is considered in its perfect state,[2] I will begin with the most perfect forms of family life and from there consider the less perfect forms. So I will first consider the nature and goal of the ideal Christian family. Next I will consider how such a family can come into existence. Finally, I shall consider the cases in which there is some imperfection or even a corruption or falling away from the ideal family and how these corruptions can be healed.

Because this work intends to treat family life briefly, it will not consider a number of important topics in detail (for example, contraception or reproductive technologies). Many of these topics have been carefully treated at length by others. This work will instead focus upon the relationships within a human family as seen from the perspective of revelation.

---

2   For example, it is easier to understand an orange tree when it is full grown than when it is in its seminal form; and it is easier to understand human nature by considering a mature human being than by considering a human being in its embryonic state.

5

On Signs about Supernatural Realities

The Lord himself shall give you a sign. (Isa. 7:14)

BEFORE ENTERING INTO A DEEPER UNDER-standing of the human family through the mysteries of our faith, we should briefly consider the need for signs and their importance in Theology. Much of what follows will argue that the human family and the relationships within it are intended by God to be signs of supernatural realities (such as the Trinity and the Incarnation). From this truth, I will argue to certain fundamental truths about the human family which come from divine revelation. The position that the family is a sign of supernatural realities is not something novel: it is something clearly found in the Scriptures and in the whole Tradition of the Church. But it may seem novel because the importance of this truth has been obscured (or at least ignored) in much recent discussion about the family. So a brief consideration of signs will be helpful as a preparation for what follows.

Because man comes to know through his senses he must use sensible things as signs of spiritual realities. The importance of signs in the intellectual and moral life of man is not inconsiderable. A sign is that which strikes the senses and brings to mind something other than itself, and so is an essential tool for the rational animal whose knowledge begins in the senses (because man is an animal) and ends in the mind (because man is rational). Some signs are natural (for example, an animal footprint is a sign of the passing of that animal, or a baby's cry is a sign that the baby is uncomfortable). Other signs are conventional: that is, they are made by human agreement (for example, traffic signs and advertisements are conventional signs). Natural signs are the same everywhere: babies' cries are understood in every culture. Conventional signs are the product of human agreement, and so differ from society to society: shaking the head means no in Europe, but yes in India. Human life is filled with both kinds of signs: some which are very obvious and others which are more subtle, like our body language which is a kind of non-verbal sign. The importance of conventional signs is most obvious from human language. Without these signs (words, statements, etc.), it is difficult if not impossible for human beings to advance in knowledge. Words are sensible signs of our invisible thoughts which in some real way reveal even our own thoughts to ourselves.[1]

God also institutes signs. Jesus teaches that the Incarnation itself is intended to be a sign when he says to Philip: "He who has seen me has seen the Father."[2] And if signs are important for the life of man in the natural order, they are even more necessary to enter into the supernatural order. Jesus says to Nicodemus: "If I tell you about earthly things and you do not believe, how will you believe if I tell you about heavenly things?"[3] In other words, if we do not understand the meaning of the natural world which God has created (earthly things) we cannot come to understand the supernatural world (heavenly things). Every word of sacred Scripture is borrowed from the natural world, so that entering into the supernatural order presupposes a knowledge and love of the natural order. We have no alternative. Signs take on an even more essential role in the supernatural life than in man's natural life, since no one in this life has a direct experience of that supernatural order: "No

---

1   Shakespeare puts this well in the words of Miranda to Caliban: "I pitied thee, took pains to make thee speak, taught thee each hour, one thing or other; when thou didst not, savage, know thine own meaning, but wouldst gabble like a thing most brutish, I endowed thy purposes with words that made them known." *The Tempest*, Act 1, Scene 2. So important are verbal signs for the life of the mind, Aristotle observes, that one born blind from birth is better off as concerns the life of the mind than one born deaf, since words are the natural signs by which we learn.

2   Jn 14:9 (NAB).

3   Jn 3:12 (NAB)

one has ever seen God."[4] Hence, that higher life is communicated to us *wholly* through signs. It follows that such signs are the only access man has to heaven. One might say that without these signs, the window to heaven is closed to us.

These sacred signs are found in their most pristine form in the seven sacraments of the Church. And of these seven sacraments, the best known is the Sacrament of Matrimony. It is best known because it is closest to nature, standing as it were on the boundary between the natural and supernatural order. And so it is the natural beginning point by which souls are lead into the life of grace. Hence, it was the first sacred sign instituted by God at the origin of our race in paradise, when he united Adam and Eve in marriage.[5] Moreover, we read in the Gospel according to St. John that it was at a wedding feast that Jesus first manifested his glory and his disciples first began to believe in him.[6] This is not by chance. The natural beginning of the Christian faith is in the Christian family, and the first sacrament by which children come to believe is the marriage between their parents. For while habitual faith is infused first at baptism, that faith becomes actual through the witness of the Sacrament of Matrimony. The Sacrament of Matrimony is the first sign by which Christ is glorified; and children first learn to believe in Christ's love for them - they first become disciples, through the marriage of their parents. And marriage is not a saving sacrament for the children only, but also for all those who shall come into intimate contact with that marriage.

In the beginning of creation, God blessed each day and called it good (cf., Gen 1). But on one occasion, it was not good: it was not good for the man to be alone. Yet once woman was made from man, God said that it was very good. Every artist has his favorite work of art, and God's favorite is the human family. From all eternity, in fact, he understood himself as the Son of Mary, as a

4   Jn 1:18 (NAB).

5   Of course, at this point, marriage was not yet a sacrament in the full sense it would later have when Christ raised it to a sign which would communicate grace by his institution.

6   See Jn 2:11.

member of a human family. The reason for God's predilection is that more than the other parts of his creation, the family reflected his own goodness and beauty. Hence, we cannot know God, we cannot love him, without knowing and loving the natural human family. To do so would be tantamount to considering someone beautiful whose accurate reflection in a mirror we consider ugly.

And so the human family is a privileged sign intended by God to lead us into supernatural realities. When we survey the principal mysteries of our faith, we find that they are expressed in terms of relationships within the human family. For example, God is a Father, who has an eternally begotten Son. This is the foundational truth of our faith. The relationship of this Son to his Church is that of a bridegroom to his bride. The love of God for his people is like that of a mother for her infant child, and so on.

Because the relationships in a human family are the first (and in some sense, only) signs by which the fundamental mysteries of the interior life of God are made known to us, it is absolutely essential that these relationships be protected, fostered and loved. For if these family relationships are distorted, destroyed or even unappreciated, this will ultimately lead to ignorance and error, indifference or even animosity, toward the entire supernatural order.

One last observation: the method which I will sometimes use in this treatise may seem backwards. For example, I will sometimes argue from this or that truth about the Trinity or the Incarnation to the conclusion that the relationships in a family should be such as to aptly signify these truths. This seems backwards because the relationships in a family are better known, so that the argument should go from the family to the mysteries of faith.

There are two principal reasons why I sometimes argue from the established truths about the mysteries of the faith to the relationships which ought to exist in a human family. First, generally speaking, in the modern world, it is not the dogmas of the faith that are being called into question. Rather it is the relationships within the family that are being challenged. From the standpoint of the modern reader, therefore, the truths of the faith are more certain, so that by showing that the two are necessarily connected, a convincing argument can be made that the relationships in a family ought to be preserved and loved.[7]

The second (and more profound) reason why I sometimes argue from the truths about the mysteries of the faith to the relationships which ought to exist within a family is because the mysteries of the faith are in themselves the cause and reason why God has established the relationships within a natural family. When going from a more-known effect to a cause, it is often helpful afterwards to look back at the effect from the perspective of its cause. For example, knowing that a lunar eclipse is caused by the interposition of the earth between the sun and the moon helps one to see more perfectly what a lunar eclipse is and its various properties. So too with the family. Knowing that the reason for the family is to reflect the light of the inner life of God helps one to understand the family itself more profoundly. *Gaudium et Spes* uses this very principle when it teaches:

> Only in the mystery of the incarnate Word does the mystery of man take on light. For Adam, the first man, was a figure of him who was to come, namely Christ the Lord. Christ, the final Adam, by the revelation of the mystery of the Father and his love, fully reveals man to man himself and makes his supreme calling clear. It is not surprising, then, that in him all the aforementioned truths find their root and attain their crown.[8]

Beholding man in the mystery of the perfect Man not only perfects our understanding of human nature because it purifies it of the stain of sin into which man has fallen, but also because it reveals the higher finality for which God designed and created human nature. This fundamental perspective about man is something to which Pope John Paul II referred over and over again in his writings. This

7 Of course, because family relationships are in themselves better known, eventually a corruption of the understanding of these family relationships will result in a corruption of the dogmas of faith (for example, understanding God as a mother instead of a Father).

8 *GS* 22.

treatise on the Theology of the family simply extends this principle from individual human nature to the family: just as the incarnate Word reveals man more fully to himself, so the mysteries of the Trinity and Incarnation reveal the family more fully to itself.

OBJECTIONS AND ANSWERS

Objection 1: There is no necessary relationship between a sign and the thing signified. For example, there is no reason why a red light should mean "stop" and a green light "go." Therefore, it is impossible to show a necessary or reasonable connection between the family and the supernatural things the family are supposed to signify.

Answer: It is true that a sign, as such, need not be connected to the thing signified except by association (as when someone associates a red light with stopping). Yet, some signs do have an essential relationship to the things signified insofar as they are likenesses of the things signified. Thus, the footprint of an animal is a likeness of the foot of that animal. In the case of the sacraments of the Church, as well as the ways in which relationships within a family signify supernatural realities, the signs are likenesses of the things signified. Thus, baptism is an outward washing, which is like the spiritual cleansing of the soul which it causes. And the relationship between a father and his son is like the relationship between God the Father and God the Son. Moreover, insofar as a sign is intended to signify the intentions of the one who uses it, the revealed truths about marriage and family give us certain knowledge of what God intends these things to signify. Therefore, even if they were not likenesses of what they signified, we could still be certain based upon the certitude of divine revelation about the connection between the divine signs and the realities they signify.

Objection 2: Words are sufficient signs of supernatural realities. Therefore, there is no need for family life to be a certain way in order to communicate a knowledge of supernatural truths. Just the words of Scripture will suffice.

Answer: Words in themselves have no meaning unless they be connected with real things in our experience. Therefore, unless someone has a direct experience of a real marriage and family, these names would remain just names without a corresponding real concept. True, the experience need not be of one's own family or marriage, but it has to be an experience of someone's family or marriage. Moreover, when someone is in a bad marriage or family, or has an experience of a corrupt or defective instance of anything, they are likely to misunderstand its true nature. The tendency would be to associate the defects with the thing in itself. For example, if your only experience of milk was spoiled milk, you might think that part of the definition of milk was to be sour tasting. As a result, someone from a defective family is much more likely to misunderstand marriage or family in itself. For instance, they might consider marriage or family to be unnatural in itself because their family or their parent's marriage had elements that were contrary to nature. Hence, it is extremely important for every person that they come from a healthy, well-ordered family if they are to accurately understand and appreciate the supernatural realities signified by these natural goods.

With these preliminaries set down, we are now in a better position to consider the family in light of the principal mysteries of our faith.

6

The Trinity as a Source of Revelation about the Family

For this reason I kneel before the Father, from whom all family in heaven and on earth is named. (Eph. 3:14-15)

THE TRINITY

One might wonder why in a book about the Theology of the family the topic of the Trinity comes up at all. St. Paul says that all family in heaven and on earth takes its name from the Father.[1] This gives a clue that the pre-eminent place where we find truth about the family is in God.

Besides this, there is another reason: a subject is understood most profoundly when it is understood in light of its first principles and causes. This is true also of the family. We know from divine revelation that the family is also a mystery which ultimately has its roots in the mystery of the Trinity. Indeed, even the terms in which the mystery of the Trinity is expressed (Father, Son) are taken from relationships which exist within a family. So the relation between the mystery of the Trinity and the mystery of the family is not remote, but rather immediate. And since the mystery of the Trinity, as the central mystery of the Christian faith, is the "source of all the other mysteries of faith, the light that enlightens them,"[2] we should consider the family in relation to this principal mystery of the Christian Faith.

I think most Catholics are used to hearing a very crude presentation of the mystery of the Trinity. If the mystery of the Trinity is taught at all, it is usually once a year on Trinity Sunday. Even

1   See Eph. 3:15.
2   CCC n.234.

115

then, it is typically taught only in very crude terms or metaphors, for example, that the Trinity is like a shamrock. This is truly a shame. The Trinity is the principal truth of our religion, and it is the primary truth Jesus came to reveal, and yet most preachers avoid speaking about the Trinity because it is difficult to speak about and difficult to understand. But the fact is that if we truly love someone, we want to know as much about that person as we can, even the things hard to understand. If a young woman married a great musician, even if she could never hope to grasp music as he does, she would still be remiss in her love if she showed little or no interest in his music. Similarly, even though we cannot hope to grasp the mystery of the inner life of God perfectly, still we would be remiss in our love if we did not strive to grasp what we can. We can do better than shamrocks.

In what follows about both the Trinity and the Incarnation, some of the explanations (though not all) presuppose a good deal of Philosophy and Theology. I have decided that it is better to include these explanations both because it will be a benefit for those who have the requisite knowledge of Philosophy and Theology, and also because the conclusions reached will be important in understanding the relationship of these great mysteries of our Faith to the family. If you do not have the background in Philosophy or Theology to understand these explanations well, don't be discouraged. You can simply look at the main conclusions and use those as a basis for understanding what follows. These main conclusions are no different than what you would expect to find in a good catechism.

In this life God can only be known by analogy to creatures, and we find the best analogy to God by considering the higher creatures: namely, the human soul and angels. Therefore, we will approach the Trinity by way of these analogies. When we know something or someone, we have an image or likeness of that thing within our soul. For example, if you were to think about your father right now, you can call to mind an image, like a photograph in your imagination, of your father. And the same thing would be true even if you thought about yourself: you would have a likeness, an image of yourself within your mind. However, that image of yourself in your mind falls short of your real self in three significant ways: first, you existed before your thought about yourself existed. Second, you are physical and have real flesh and bones, while the image in your mind is spiritual, and does not have physical matter. Third, your thoughts exist in you and depend upon you to exist, while the real you exists on its own and not in dependence upon another.

So in human knowing, there is a large difference between the thing known and the image or likeness in the mind of the knower. But in angels, this difference is less. When an angel is thinking about himself, that angel also has a likeness of himself in his understanding. But since angels are in some sense outside of time, their thought about themselves comes into being simultaneously with their own existence. Not only that, but an angel is spiritual, not physical or material, so the second difference between his thought and the thing he knows does not exist: the thing he is thinking about is spiritual, and his thought is also spiritual. They are alike in this respect. But the third difference still remains: the angel is more real than his thoughts. His thought depends upon his mind to exist, but the real angel does not depend upon his mind or his thought to exist, but rather the converse is true. So even if the angel were to think about himself, there would still be a big difference between an angel and his thought about himself.

But when we get to God, all three differences disappear. First of all, God is altogether outside of time, so that his concept of himself is co-eternal with him. Moreover, both God's concept and his own being are spiritual, not physical. Finally, since in God everything is as real and perfect as it can be and nothing in him is caused, God's concept of himself would not be dependent upon something else: it must have existence in itself. So the third difference disappears as well. Therefore, God's own concept of himself would be identical to himself in every way. We rightly call this divine conception the Word of God as well as the Son of God: for the Word which is conceived is a living being of the same nature as the One from whom he proceeds. And since God has had this concept of himself for all eternity, there was never a time in which this concept did not exist in God. This is what we mean when we say that the Son is eternally-begotten of the Father: the conceiving of the Son is an eternal activity, always taking place in the single moment of God's everlasting present. Since the Word is identical in every way to the Father who conceives him, we affirm in the creed that he is God from God, Light from Light, true God from true God, begotten not made, consubstantial with the Father.

And since together with every act of knowing, there is a corresponding act of love, we find also in God a movement of love, a procession through which a third Person is understood to be constituted. This new procession terminates in a new relation which is really distinct from both the Father and the Son. This third Person is called Love because of the way in which he proceeds from the Father and the Son. In Scripture he is also called the Holy Spirit by way of a certain analogy. Just as the second Person of the Trinity is called the Word by analogy to the spoken word which signifies the truth conceived in the mind, so also the third Person of the Trinity is called the Spirit by analogy to a word which is spoken in love. Such a word is not merely spoken, but breathed forth in the way that the lover sighs in speaking about his beloved. With the Father and the Son, the Holy Spirit is one God, fully possessing the same, identical, divine substance. The Holy Spirit proceeds from the Father and the Son as from a single principle, since they are not related to the Spirit in two different ways. The western Church expresses this procession in the *Filioque*–that is, the assertion in the Creed that the Holy Spirit proceeds from the Father and the Son. So there is a brief account of how we might better understand the Persons of the Trinity by analogy to the activities of the human soul.

To recapitulate using more formal language we can say that the Catholic Faith teaches that in the one God there exist three really distinct divine Persons. Each of these Persons is fully divine and identical with the divine substance, but really distinct from one another on account of their real relations of origin.[3] Everything in them is one where there is no opposition of relationship.[4]

---

3   CCC n.254.
4   Council of Florence (1442): DS 1330.

This account of the Trinity should not be considered a comprehensive and perfect explanation of the mystery of the Trinity. It is an approach to this mystery by way of analogy. Yet it is an analogy based upon the very words used in divine revelation. God chose to reveal himself using human words, and those words have determinate meanings in human discourse. God is revealed as Father, as Word and Son, as Spirit and Love. The Son is said to proceed from the Father[5] and to be toward the Father.[6] God chose these words and not others precisely because they approach most closely to the whole truth about his inner life. We are not free to discard these words or to use others in their place. The Church and her authoritative teachers have carefully considered these words and distinguished their meanings. The above account in terms of the activities of the intellect and will most clearly and perfectly articulate the analogy which exists between God and creatures. Therefore, while this account is not to be considered comprehensive and perfect, still it is perennial and cannot be discarded as if it were merely provisional. We will always have to approach the divine mysteries through these words.

OBJECTIONS AND ANSWERS

Objection 1: It is a contradiction to say that the Father is identical with the divine substance, and the Son is identical with the same divine substance, yet the Father is not identical with the Son. If two things are the same as a third thing, they must be the same as each other.

Answer: The Father is the divine substance insofar as it begets or conceives, but the Son is that same divine substance insofar as it is begotten or conceived. And so they cannot be identified with each other, even though they are the same substance. Take a parallel example: the Morning Star is the planet Venus insofar as it rises before the Sun, and the Evening Star is the same planet Venus insofar as it sets after the Sun. But from this we cannot identify the

5   Jn. 8:42.
6   Jn. 1:1.

Morning Star with the Evening Star. For example, it is not true to say that the Evening Star rises before the Sun, but it is true to say that the Morning Star rises before the Sun. They are the same in substance, but they bear a different relationship to the Sun, and hence cannot be identified with each other insofar as they have this opposed relationship. Similarly, the Father and Son are the same in substance, yet cannot be identified with each other insofar as they have an opposed relationship, namely the relationship of begetter and begotten.

Objection 2: The Father and the Son seem to differ only in our way of thinking about them, not really in themselves.

Answer: This position would be the heresy of modalism. Modalism treats the relationship of begetter and begotten as if it were just in our mind, but not something real in God. But begetting and being begotten are real in God, not just in our way of thinking about God. This is clear from the Scriptures which treat the Father, Son and Holy Spirit as really distinct Persons: "And when Jesus was baptized, he went up immediately from the water, and behold, the heavens were opened and he saw the Spirit of God descending like a dove, and alighting on him; and lo, a voice from heaven, saying: 'This is my beloved Son, with whom I am well pleased.'"[7]

Objection 3: If we mean anything by the name God, we mean the first cause which is not caused by anything else. But if God is begotten, it seems to follow that God derives his existence from a prior cause, and so he is not God after all.

Answer: When animals are begotten, they depend for their coming to be from their begetter. But the word "begotten" is not used in that sense in God. Recall that in God, the begetting is purely spiritual, in the way someone forms a concept. Recall too that in God, this concept does not depend upon something for its existence the way our concepts do. And so the concept begotten in God does not depend upon anything either for its being or coming to be.

7   Matt 3:16-17 (RSV).

To be begotten in God means simply to be from another and in relation to that other, but not in such a way as to depend upon that other for existence. Both begetter and begotten exist in simultaneous relationship to one another, like the knower and the thing known, where neither side of the relationship depends upon the other, but both are equal to one another.

THE TRINITARIAN COMMUNION

One reason why the Trinity is the exemplar of family life is because the communion found in family life has its supreme model and source in the communion among the Persons of the Trinity.[8] St. John tells us that within God there is a communion and that we are called to enter into that communion: "That which we have seen and heard we proclaim also to you, so that you may have communion with us; and our communion is with the Father and with his Son Jesus Christ."[9]

On this account, is it correct to call the Trinity a family? Not in the same sense in which a human family is a family. Yet the communion among the Persons in the Trinity has a likeness and proportion to the communion found within a family. Both the Trinity and the family can be called a communion of persons. But what is this communion, and why are we called by God to enter into it?

To understand the meaning of the term communion more precisely, it may help to compare it to a similar concept: community. A community is a multitude of persons all united by a single purpose or good. For example, the city of Pasadena is a community but it is not a communion. For many persons in the city of Pasadena are not even aware of one another's existence, so they do not know or love one another. In contrast, both a family and a friendship are communions. The persons in a family or a friendship do not merely have a common goal or good to achieve, they know one another intimately, and care about each other, and live together. As Aristotle famously

8 "God is love, and in himself he lives a mystery of personal, loving communion." *Familiaris Consortio* 11.

9 1 Jn 1:3 (NAB).

observed, a friend is another self. So a communion can be defined as *a multitude of persons in which each person somehow lives the life of every other person*. Both within the Trinity and within a family, we find communion. The fact that God chose to reveal himself as Father and Son also points to the likeness between the communion found in a family and the communion found among the Persons in God. However, within the Trinity we find the supreme and most perfect communion: for the divine Persons live the selfsame life in an utterly undivided way.

What does it mean to share or live the life of another person? What does it mean to enter into communion with another person? To answer this question, we must first answer a more fundamental question: "what is life?" For communion means sharing a life with another. To live is to have within oneself an active principle of self-motion. Inanimate things and dead things are moved from the outside. They do not move themselves, or sense or even grow or take in food. Among living things we find a certain gradation. Some, like plants, only grow, take in nutrition and reproduce. Others, like animals, also sense and move themselves from place to place. Still others, like men, are capable of understanding and loving. The higher up this scale we move, the more apparent and perfect life seems to be.

Life in ourselves is something very real and well known. Life in plants, especially the lower plants like fungi, or imperfect plants, like seeds, is not very apparent, and they seem like non-living things in many respects. The reason for this experience is that the living activities found in higher life forms more fully realize what life is: they are more truly active and more truly self-movers, since they depend less upon other things in order to act. Nutrition and growth in plants looks almost mechanical, and seems to be largely passive and dependent upon the external environment.

Sensation on the other hand seems to be more active and interior and less dependent upon external things. But even sensation depends upon material bodies. We cannot sense heat unless our flesh undergoes a physical alteration. This fact causes some to wonder whether sensing heat for an animal is really different than what happens in something which is non-living (e.g., a heat sensor). Moreover, sensation is also largely passive, since it requires an external sense object to act upon the sense organ. Color for example, is necessary to move the eye: we cannot see at will; heat is necessary to affect our sense of touch, we cannot feel heat at will.

But in understanding and loving, the object of our understanding is wholly interior and our ability to understand and love does not demand the external presence of the object. So more than these other activities, understanding and loving are truly living activities. This is why we consider them more essential to our life and to our person. No sane person would choose to lose his senses (e.g., to be in a coma) in order to gain the longevity of a redwood. And if we had to choose between losing our eyesight or our mind, no one would choose to lose their mind. We consider the life of our mind to be most truly our life.

Paradoxically, the interiority and independence characteristic of life does not isolate a living thing from other things. In fact, the more perfectly a living thing possesses life, the more perfectly is it able to enter into relationship with other things. The plant in virtue of its life is enabled to beget a distinct individual of the same kind whenever it reproduces. Going beyond this, an animal is able to somehow take in the outward qualities of things around it through its senses. As a consequence, animals are aware of their surroundings and are enabled to consciously interact with other beings, especially members of their own species. The rational being is able to exceed the awareness which mere sensation provides so as to receive the very substance of other things, by knowing what they are. This is why Aristotle called the soul the "place of forms" since the forms of all things are somehow able to exist simultaneously within the soul of a knower. The possession of another through knowledge begets an inclination for a more perfect union with that other through love. So another mark of life is that living things are able to enter into relationships with other beings, and the more perfect is their life, the more perfect is the relationship established with others. This is a reflection of the relations existing in the Trinity. Self-movement and self-possession makes communion possible since nothing gives what it does not possess, and communion at its highest level involves giving oneself: "The good is diffusive of itself."[10]

We are now in a better position to consider the question about communion among the persons of the Trinity. To do this we need to understand better what it means to say that God has life. The life of God is best understood by analogy to our life of understanding and loving. God does not grow or eat like a plant, nor does he have bodily senses like sight or smell, like an animal. But God does understand and love in a way more perfect than (yet analogous to) the way we understand and love. In fact, as St. Thomas teaches: "Life is most properly found in God."[11] Since life is found above all in the activities of knowing and loving, and since these activities are the foundation for our understanding of the relations in God, it is manifest that communion is found in the Trinity in the highest degree. Unlike human persons, the relations of the divine Persons are essentially determined by the processions of knowledge and love. Knowledge and love are most intimately bound up with the divine Persons.

In addition to this difference between the communion of the divine Persons and human persons, there are others. Human knowledge and love, though it is truly free and self-active, still involves dependence upon external things for its activity. For example, our knowledge begins from certain self-evident principles which are determined by nature, and our will naturally seeks happiness. Both the beginnings of our knowledge and the ultimate end of our desires is something determined for us by the one who established our human nature. So our activities of knowing and loving are not wholly independent of external causes. So human life is not active or self-moving in the most perfect way. But God does not have any

10   This axiom found especially among scholastic Philosophers means that to the degree that something is good and perfect, so does it communicate its goodness and perfection to others. Wise men naturally communicate truth in greater abundance to others. Virtuous men naturally attract others towards goodness, etc.

11   *Summa Theologia*, Ia, q.18, a.3, c.

external causes responsible for his activities of knowledge or love. He is fully active, free, independent and self-responsible, and so God is most truly and properly alive.

Since God most perfectly possesses himself and "moves"[12] himself, he is most able to give himself and enter into communion with another. This is what happens in the divine processions: by a wholly interior intellectual act, a really distinct divine Person (the Son) eternally proceeds who is at once entirely from another, and in relationship with the one from whom he proceeds (the Father), yet independent, and self-possessed of divine life as much as the one from whom he receives it. And in like manner, by a wholly interior act of love, the Holy Spirit proceeds from the Father and the Son. So perfect is the relationship constituted by this sharing of life that the very personhood of each divine Person is identical with the relationship constituted by the active processions.

In contrast to the divine gift of self, a creature is able to give itself and enter into communion with another only in virtue of being moved to do so by some extrinsic cause or principle. We might say that the communion of a created person is that of a given giver: one who can give only because he has received the power to give from another: "We love because he first loved us;"[13] "It was not you who chose me, but I who chose you."[14] As a consequence of this, the gift of self which marks created communions is not a definitive gift in which the receiver can finally rest, but it points to a prior giving. And only this prior gift is able to bring the soul to rest: "You have made us for yourself O Lord, and our hearts are restless until they rest in you."[15]

Another way in which the Trinitarian communion surpasses the communion among creatures is the manner in which their life is shared. Each of the three Persons is living the very same, individual, divine life. They are not each sharing part of this life, but each

12   As applied to God, the term "moves" does not imply change, but rather perfect activity.

13   1 Jn 4:19 (NAB).

14   Jn 15:16 (NAB).

15   St. Augustine, *Confessions* I.1.

lives the entirety of the selfsame divine life. Each saint in heaven has a different vision of God (which is why those visions can be unequal). But the Father's understanding of himself is not really distinct from the Son's understanding of himself, nor is their love for one another distinct from the Holy Spirit's love for them. So when we say that the Persons of the Trinity have a common life, it is not a matter of participation, since each person possesses that divine life wholly and completely, and not in any sense as a "part" (as the name participation implies). Moreover, in God this communion of life is uninterrupted and eternal.

The way in which created persons share their lives is imperfect compared to the way in which this takes place in God. Created persons do not live the same, individual life. Their life is shared by way of participation, in which each person somehow lives a part of the life of another, but not the whole of it. Even so, in a profound communion, there is a tendency to share as much of one's life as possible.[16] Imperfect communion strives to be like its divine model to the extent that it is able. This is especially evident in families, in which the father and mother see their own natures and life principle communicated to their children, and children see their lives as being from their father and mother.[17] The begetting of children allows one to understand experientially something of the inner life of God.

In his Apostolic Letter *Mulieris Dignitatem*, Pope John Paul II forcefully makes the point that we are called to enter into a likeness of the divine communion by asserting the connection between inter-personal communion (especially spousal communion) and the fact that man has been made in the image of God:

---

16   This is why, for example, friends like to share memories or photographs of their past lives with one another, prior to the time they first met. It is as if their friend is somehow enabled in this way to go back and live that part of their life with them.

17   I have often seen how becoming a parent transforms the interior life of a Christian. They begin to understand more perfectly how God loves them and provides for them. They are better able to see their relationship with God from God's perspective.

Every individual is made in the image of God, insofar as he or she is a rational and free creature capable of knowing God and loving him. Moreover, we read that man cannot exist "alone" (cf. Gen. 2:18); he can exist only as a "unity of the two," and therefore *in relation to another human person*. It is a question here of a mutual relationship: man to woman, woman to man. Being a person in the image and likeness of God thus also involves existing in a relationship, in relation to the other "I." This is a prelude to the definitive self-revelation of the Triune God: a living unity in the communion of the Father, Son and Holy Spirit.[18]

He goes on to say a little later:

The model for this interpretation of the person is God himself as Trinity, as a communion of Persons. To say that man is created in the image and likeness of God means that man is called to exist "for" others, to become a gift.[19]

This is not to assert in an unqualified way that the relationship itself between two spouses or persons in communion are in the image of the Triune God.[20] Rather, it is to point out that

18   Pope John Paul II, *Mulieris Dignitatem* (1988), pgh.7.
19   *Ibid*.
20   St. Thomas shows that the family is not made in the image of God, but rather the mind of the individual person is: *Summa Theologica*, I, q.93, a.6, ad.2. In addition to this, it can also be shown that the image of God is not found in the relationship of communion between two created persons. The notion of one thing having the image of another requires not only generic likeness, but also specific likeness. Within the individual soul, the acts of knowing and loving God involve this specific likeness. But the relationship of communion between two created persons, while it involves knowing and loving between them, is not specifically like the relationships among the Persons of the Trinity for three reasons. First, the object of knowledge and love is outside, rather than inside the nature of the one knowing and loving (*S. T.*, I, q.93, a.6, ad.4); second, the divine nature is not the object of the activities of knowledge and love (*S. T.*, q.93, a.8); third, the term of these two processions of knowledge and love are the same person, not distinct persons.

inter-personal communion is a direct and necessary consequence of the image of God found within each person. The activities of knowing and loving God in the mind of each individual, human person (according to which each person is said to be in the image of God) falls short of the full reality found in the Trinity, wherein the terms of the processions of knowledge and love are distinct and real persons. So as a way of supplementing this shortcoming, man enters into communion with other, real persons (albeit, persons outside of his own being and nature). To the extent that he is able, man strives to experience life and communion in a way that is conformed to the life and communion found in the Trinity of Persons.

In summary, the divine communion is most perfect both because the kind of life God lives is most perfect, and because the way in which this same life is lived by the divine Persons is most perfect. Yet the very perfection of the divine life, unattainable as it is for creatures, serves as a goal towards which the communion among created persons must strive to reach its highest perfection. Communion among created persons, especially communion within a family, is found most perfectly where the life of each person is most freely given to and completely shared with the other persons in that communion.

OBJECTIONS AND ANSWERS

Objection 1: The communion among the persons of the Trinity is not exactly like the communion between spouses or between parents and children, therefore, the communion of family life is not an apt analogy of the communion of the Trinity.

Answer: In human knowledge, we must always move from what is better known to what is less well known. The communion within a family is not only better known to us than the communion within the Trinity (no one has seen God), it is the natural communion which is most analogous to the communion within the Trinity. We know this through divine revelation from someone who experienced that Trinitarian communion first-hand: Jesus Christ. For one thing to be analogous with another thing it is not required that they be alike in every respect. Every analogy limps. If they were alike in every respect, they would no longer be analogous, but the same thing.

Objection 2: The Trinity is not a family according to the same definition we have given. For example, there is no husband and wife in the Trinity. Therefore, a different definition of family will not have any negative consequences for understanding the Trinity.

Answer: While the definition of the family does not apply to the Trinity, it does not follow from this that a new definition of family will not impede our knowledge of the Trinity. For while the definition of family is not applied, even analogously to the Trinity, nevertheless, the relationships within a family are the primary analogates in terms of which we understand the relationships within the Trinity. And so since changing the definition of family necessarily means changing the relationships within a family, it follows that changing the definition of family will impede our knowledge of the Trinity.

Objection 3: Marriage is a sign of the union of the divine and the human in the Incarnation. But marriage is not included in any dogmatic definitions about the Incarnation. In fact, the Incarnation seems to be perfectly understandable without understanding marriage at all. Therefore, for a similar reason, the relationship between a father and his son is in no way essential for understanding the mystery of the Trinity.

Answer: The case of marriage as a means of knowing the Incarnation is not the same as the case of the relation between father and son as a means of knowing the Trinity. Marriage leads to a knowledge of the Incarnation by way of likeness, while the relationship between father and son leads to the knowledge of the Trinity by way of proper analogy.[21] For this reason the concepts of Father and Son

21 An analogy between two things implies not merely some likeness, but a proportion sufficient to lead the mind from one to the other. Two things can be alike in many respects, yet not be sufficient to lead the mind from one to the other. A sign of this is that the very same thing may have a likeness to two opposite things. For example, a lion is like Christ on account of strength and

are included in the very definition of the Trinity. The very best analogy which Christ could give us about the relationship between his Person and the Person from whom he proceeds is the relationship between a father and his son. Therefore, an accurate knowledge of the Trinity would be impossible without knowing the relationship between father and son. The fact that marriage leads to a knowledge of the Incarnation only by way of likeness does not mean, however, that marriage is a dispensable sign of the union of the divine and the human.[22]

---

daring, but it is like the devil on account of cruelty. Hence, the Scriptures call both Christ and the devil lions: the lion of the tribe of Judah (Rev. 5:5); the devil prowls like a roaring lion (1 Pet. 5:8). Proper analogies, however, are able to lead the mind from one concept to another so as to communicate certain knowledge. For example, the act of the eye is analogous to the act of the mind, and from understanding "seeing" of the eye, we can be lead to possess certain knowledge about "seeing" of the mind.

22   See the answer to objection 3 in chapter 7 below.

7

The Incarnation as Source of Revelation about the Family

MAN'S COMMUNION WITH GOD TAKES PLACE most perfectly through the mystery of the Incarnation. The prophet Isaiah describes the union of God with his people in terms of a marriage: "As a young man marries a virgin, your Builder shall marry you; and as a bridegroom rejoices in his bride so shall your God rejoice in you"[1] Marriage implies a union of flesh: "The two shall become one flesh"[2] This union "in the flesh" between man and God prophesied by Isaiah takes place at the moment of the Incarnation: "The Word became flesh and made his dwelling among us."[3]

The intimacy of union between human nature and the divine nature in the Person of Jesus Christ is so profound, that it can be said without qualification that this man, Jesus Christ is God; or, put another way, the Person Jesus Christ is fully human and fully divine. The Person of the Word "stands under" (in Greek hypo-stasis) both the divine nature and the human nature, which is why the union is called the hypostatic union, namely a union in one Person who is the ultimate subject standing under both natures.

One consequence of the hypostatic union is that God and man can share the same life. The act of existence which is the ultimate ground of being for the human nature of Christ is the divine act of existence, and this act of existence is identical to the divine life. So Christ exists in and by the divine life. So Christ can be said to

---

1 Isa 62:5 (NAB).
2 Mk 10:8 (NAB).
3 Jn 1:14 (NAB).

be God and to live by the life of God, even in his human nature. Moreover, the sharing of life at the level of being extends to a sharing of life at the level of activity. Thus St. Leo the Great wrote: "Each nature exercises its own activity in communion with the other."[4]

Still, Christ has a fully human nature, and this nature is the principle of properly human living powers and activities. He has a human soul, with a human intellect and will, human emotions and sensations, even human powers of nutrition. Yet whenever he exercises these powers, it is properly speaking the Person of the Word who knows, who loves, who suffers, who eats. Natures do not act or live: a nature is *that by which* something lives or acts. It is rather the ultimate subject of a nature, the thing which *has* a nature, that lives or acts. Humanity does not live or think or love; rather a person *having* humanity lives and thinks and loves. So too the human living activities of Christ are the living acts of the Person of the Word. God the Son lives a human life through his human nature, and he lives a divine life through his divine nature. Human beings experience something analogous to this since we have two fundamentally different ways of living: sense life and intellectual life. And just as we are said to be living one life whether we live through our intellective power or our sense power, so also Christ is living one life through both his divine and human natures. As a consequence, the communion between the human and divine is found most perfectly in Christ: in one Person, the divine life and the human life are perfectly shared.[5]

THE INCARNATION AS SIGN AND THING SIGNIFIED

Through Christ, we enter into this sharing of life. By being incorporated into Christ through the sacraments of Baptism and the Eucharist, we are made partakers of the divine life of Jesus, as he

---

4   Epist. 28 ad Flavianum, (PL 54).

5   Notice that the definition of communion given above does not strictly apply to the case of the Incarnation since in the Incarnation there is not a "multitude of persons." But in the Incarnation there is something more perfect than communion, just as the unity a man has with himself is more perfect than the union he has with his friend.

teaches: "Just as the living Father sent me and I have life because of the Father, so also the one who feeds on me will have life because of me."[6] The sacraments extend the power of Christ's Incarnation and communicate it to human souls through bodily and outward signs. Hence, we enter into the communion of the Trinitarian life through the instrumentality of the Incarnation and the sacraments. In this way, we become members of God's family, children of the Father and brothers and sisters of the Son.[7]

The Incarnation is both a sign which reveals and allows us to enter into the Trinitarian communion, and something signified by the communion which exists within a human family. Marriage, which is the foundational relationship of communion within a family, is itself a sacrament of the union of the divine and human in the Incarnation: "The Christian conjugal bond . . . represents the mystery of Christ's Incarnation."[8] So we can now define marriage as a sacrament: marriage as a sacrament is *a lifelong communion of a man and woman, established by their free consent, for the sake of the generation and education of children, and which is intended by God to be a sign of the union of the divine and human in order to communicate the very grace of union which it signifies.* There are many likenesses between sacramental marriage and the hypostatic union which make the former a fitting sign of the latter:

> 1) First, both are unions between different yet complementary elements.
>
> 2) Second, as the divine and human are united in a single person, so in a similar manner the union of marriage forms one "moral person;"[9] so much so that

6   Jn 6:57 (NAB)

7   Cf., Jn 1:12.

8   *Familiaris Consortio* 13.

9   Of course, there is a dissimilarity here between marriage and the Incarnation to the extent that in a marriage the union is between two physical persons, as St. Gregory cautions: "But far be it from us to conclude that because marriage takes place between two separate persons, that therefore the Person of our Redeemer was made up of two separate persons." *On the Gospels* (Mt 22:1-13), n.3.

the Scriptures many times assert that they become "one flesh."[10]

3) Third, just as in marriage one man is united to one woman, so in the hypostatic union, one divine nature is united to one human nature.

4) Fourth, just as the union between spouses in marriage is effected by the consent of the spouses, so also a certain consent was given at the Incarnation.[11]

5) Fifth, both unions are indissoluble.

6) Sixth, marriage is a union in which spouses share a life. So too in the Incarnation, the human and divine natures share a life, as I have described above.

7) Seventh, in marriage spouses cooperate to beget new life. So also in the Incarnation the human and divine natures cooperate to beget new life: "From his fullness we have all received;"[12] "Shall I that give generation to others be barren saith the Lord thy God?"[13]

On account of these likenesses, one can see more clearly how marriage is intended to signify the mystery of the Incarnation. Marriage as a sacrament has the purpose of revealing these truths about the Incarnation. This means that one of the ends or "final causes"[14] of marriage is to signify clearly the truth about the Incarnation.

---

10   Cf. Gen 2:24; Matt 19:6; Mk 10:8; Eph. 5:31; and 1 Cor 6:16. In its primary sense, this assertion can be taken to mean that according to the inclination of the will, spouses are inclined to treat one another as they do their own bodies (cf. Eph. 5:28-29). In a secondary sense, it may also be taken to refer to the effect of their union, namely children, who unite in themselves, the flesh of their parents.

11   *S. T.*, IIIa, q.30, a.1: "It was fitting that the conception of Christ be announced to the blessed Virgin . . . in order to manifest a certain spiritual matrimony between the Son of God and human nature. And therefore, through the Annunciation the consent of the Virgin was sought on behalf of all human nature."

12   Jn 1:16 (NAB).

13   Isa 66:9 (DR).

14   A "final cause" is one of the four kinds of causes we find in ordinary experience. It is the reason for the sake of which something comes to be or exists. For example, the final cause of a knife is to cut and the final cause of a pen is to write.

In the Scriptures and in the theological tradition of the Church, marriage was first of all seen as a sacrament of the union between Christ and the Church: "'For this reason a man shall leave (his) father and (his) mother and be joined to his wife, and the two shall become one flesh.' This is a great mystery, but I speak in reference to Christ and the Church."[15] But more profound theological reflection leads to the understanding of marriage also as a sign of the hypostatic union. Augustine says, for example: "The nuptial union is effected between the Word and human flesh, and the place where the union is consummated is the Virgin's womb."[16] Gregory the Great also teaches: "God the Father made a marriage feast for God the Son when he joined him to human nature in the womb of the Virgin."[17] Indeed, the union of Christ and his Church itself finds its archetype and cause in the hypostatic union, which is why St. Paul alternately refers to the Church as both the bride and body of Christ. St. Thomas goes so far as to ground the inseparability of sacramental marriage upon the hypostatic union: "This inseparability of matrimony is principally caused inasmuch as it is a sacrament of the indissoluble conjunction of Christ and the Church, or of the Word and human nature in the Person of Christ."[18] The reason he can make this claim is precisely because St. Thomas sees the signification of the Incarnation as one of the final causes for which marriage was instituted. Pope John Paul II teaches this as the doctrine of the Church when he states: "This revelation [of the original truth of marriage] reaches its definitive fullness in the gift of love which the Word of God makes to humanity in assuming a human nature."[19]

We can extend St. Thomas' argument to include the other likenesses by which marriage is an apt sign of the hypostatic union. For example,

15 Eph 5:31-32 (NAB). In fact, the primary analogy for the Incarnation used by the Fathers was the union between soul and body.

16 Exposition of Psalm 44, n.3. See also Augustine's Sermon on the Birth of John the Baptist (PL 38:1319).

17 *On the Gospels* (Mt 22:1-13), n.3.

18 *Super Rom.*, c.7, lect.1. Also, see *Familiaris Consortio* 13: "By virtue of the sacramentality of their marriage, spouses are bound to one another in the most profoundly indissoluble manner."

19 *Familiaris Consortio* 13.

we can conclude that the communion of life between the divinity and humanity of the Incarnate Word is the cause of the communion of life between married spouses. Why should spouses share a life together and live in communion? Because one of the purposes for which marriage was instituted was to signify the communion between the human and divine life in the Incarnate Word. To the extent that spouses share a more intimate communion, to the same extent is that marriage more able to communicate and reveal the intimate communion between the human and divine natures of Christ.

Similarly, the fruitfulness of the hypostatic union is the cause why marriage should be ordained to begetting new life. St. John in his prologue argues that the divine life is communicated to men through the humanity of Christ, as he states in his first Epistle: "God sent his only Son into the world so that we might have life through him."[20] That this life is communicated through his human nature is made even more evident in the Eucharistic discourse: "Just as the living Father sent me and I have life because of the Father, so also the one who feeds on me will have life because of me."[21] Marriage was instituted to signify the communication of life by means of the union of the human with the divine. Therefore, the reason why marriage should be ordained to begetting new life is to reveal this aspect of the mystery of the Incarnation.

Again, the fact that the hypostatic union is a union between different yet complementary elements: divinity and humanity in which one is giving and active while the other is receptive is signified by the complementary difference between man and woman.[22] So again, as a sacrament, the hypostatic union is the cause of why marriage must be between a man and a woman. Finally, the fact that only one divine and one human nature are united in the Incarnation is the cause why only one man and one woman are united in the Sacrament of Matrimony.

20   1 Jn 4:9 (NAB).

21   Jn 6:57 (NAB).

22   Of course, man and woman are equal in nature, which is not true about the divine and human nature. Still the relation of active to receptive is an apt sign of the relationship between the divine and human in Christ.

The above considerations have focused upon marriage as a sacrament instituted by Christ, but in fact, marriage can be considered both as something natural and as a sacrament instituted by Christ to communicate grace. And insofar as marriage is something natural, before Christ's institution, it was already a kind of natural sacrament (though a sacrament in an analogous sense). St. Thomas asserts that "it was necessary before the coming of Christ that there be certain visible signs by which man might express his faith about the future coming of the savior. And signs of this kind are called sacraments."[23] Yet before Christ, matrimony was not a sacrament in the same sense that the seven sacraments of the new law are sacraments: "matrimony was instituted in the state of innocence not according as it was a sacrament, but according as it is for a duty of nature. Yet, consequently it signified something future about Christ and the Church."[24] However, natural marriage before Christ was a sacrament in an analogous sense: "Before the written law, there were certain sacraments of necessity just as that sacrament of faith which was ordained to the removal of original sin; and similarly, penance which was ordained to the removal of actual sin; and likewise matrimony which was ordained to the multiplication of the human race."[25]

By means of human reason, only a part of the meaning and significance of marriage could be discovered. But after the coming of Christ, the full meaning of marriage as a sign of the Incarnation and also the communion of Christ and his Church was revealed. This means that even a non-sacramental, natural marriage has a certain dignity and worth because of its suitability and intrinsic orientation to signify and make known heavenly realities. The Fathers of the Church used to say about the Church of Christ: *extra Ecclesiam nulla salus*, so also it can be said without exaggeration that *extra familiam nulla salus*. For no one is saved without the witness of a faithful Christian family: either their own, or someone else's. The family is the seed and germ of the Church.

23   *S. T.*, IIIa, q.61, a.3, c.
24   *S. T.*, IIIa, q.61, a.2, ad.3.
25   *In IV Sent.*, d.1, q.1, a.2c, ad.2.

CHRIST THE BRIDEGROOM AND
THE CHURCH HIS BRIDE:

As mentioned above, the principal mystery signified by the sacrament of marriage in the theological tradition of the Church is the mystery of the relationship between Christ and his Church. This truth is directly asserted in the Scriptures. Christ refers to himself as the "Bridegroom."[26] And St. Paul teaches: "'For this reason a man shall leave (his) father and (his) mother and be joined to his wife, and the two shall become one flesh.' This is a great mystery, but I speak in reference to Christ and the Church."[27] Once again, there are many likenesses between marriage and the union of Christ with his Church:

1) First, as the union between Christ and his Church was initiated by the sacrificial love of Christ, so also the union between husband and wife is initiated by the sacrificial love of the husband for his wife: "Christ loved the Church and handed himself over for her."[28]

2) Second, as the husband is inseparably united to his wife, so Christ is inseparably united to his Church.

3) Third, as the vows which spouses make to one another are not conditional, that is, they are binding even if the other spouse is unfaithful, so too the love of Christ for the Church is not conditional: "If we are unfaithful he remains faithful, for he cannot deny himself."[29]

4) Fourth, as a husband has only one wife, so Christ has only one Church.

5) Fifth, as a husband and wife share in one life, so too Christ communicates his own life to the Church: "From his fullness we have all received."[30]

6) Sixth, as the husband is the head of his wife, so Christ is the head of the Church: "The husband is head

---

26   Mt 9:15; Mk 2:19-20; Lk 5:34-35.
27   Eph 5:31-32 (NAB).
28   Eph 5:25 (NAB); Cf. 1 Jn 4:19.
29   2 Tim 2:13 (NAB).
30   Jn 1:16 (NAB).

of his wife just as Christ is head of the Church, he himself the savior of the body. As the Church is subordinate to Christ, so wives should be subordinate to their husbands in everything."[31]

7) Seventh, as Christ in an act of love begets new faithful through and in his Church, so a husband in an act of love begets children through and in his wife.

8) Eighth, as a husband rejoices over his bride, so Christ rejoices over his Church when she is finally inseparably united to him in Heaven: "As a bridegroom rejoices in his bride, so shall your God rejoice in you."[32]

St. Paul uses many of these likenesses between marriage and the union of Christ to his Church in order to manifest how husbands and wives ought to relate to one another. Their marriage is intended by God to be a sign of this union of Christ to his Church, and therefore, this significance is the cause or purpose why husbands and wives ought to relate to one another in this way.

THE LOVE OF THE HUSBAND

The communion between husband and wife begins with the love of the husband. It is the young man who initiates a courtship and the young man who proposes marriage. This is not just a cultural convention: it is a natural inclination that is meant to signify the initiative of Christ's love for his Church. St. John Chrysostom says that a husband should be willing to be cut into ten-thousand pieces for his wife.[33] This is in imitation of Christ's love for the Church. And the willingness to suffer for his wife does not only involve suffering at the hands of those outside, but even when it is his wife herself who is the cause of his suffering. For Christ died for us "while we were still sinners."[34] Christ suffered at the hands of those who were and would be members of his Church.

---

31   Eph 5:23-24 (NAB).
32   Isa 62:5 (NAB).
33   Homily 20 on Ephesians.
34   Rom 5:8 (NAB).

THE AUTHORITY OF THE HUSBAND

In response to the love of her husband, the wife is called to be subject to her husband. This is a very unpopular teaching today, but it is inescapably revealed in the Scriptures. And the truth is, in spite of the cultural bias against this teaching, a wife will find it easy to be subject to her husband when she knows that he loves her as himself. For she will be secure that his choices arise from a genuine desire and will for her good and the good of the family. This subjection is not one of servitude, but one which involves mutual respect and consideration. When legitimate disagreements occur between spouses, they should discuss it reasonably, and often the wife has the more reasonable position. In such cases, the husband ought to defer to his wife's position. But sometimes even two reasonable persons can be at an impasse, where no agreement can be reached. And in a family, there are only two parents. There is no tie-breaker vote. If the unity of the family is to be assured, it is necessary that when such an impasse takes place, there be a final authority for making important decisions which bear upon family life. And it is a revealed truth that this authority belongs to the husband. This is not because the husband is smarter, or holier than his wife. Even in the Holy Family this was not the case. The reason why the authority belongs to the husband is because he is a sign of Christ who is head of the Church. As a consequence of this, God guarantees that he will guide the husband's choices by his special providence.[35]

This being said, it must be reiterated that the husband does not bear authority over his wife in the way that a parent has authority

---

35   By way of anecdotal support for this thesis, I have personally seen many cases where God works though the husband in an extraordinary manner when the husband and wife have disagreed. In one case, a young woman was having her first child. A few months before she was due, she started to itch, sometimes even on her palms. She mentioned it to her husband without much concern. But the husband was very concerned and began to research the symptoms. He discovered a rare and potentially fatal condition which could have matched her symptoms, but it was so rare that the wife did not want to spend the money or time seeing a doctor about it. But the husband insisted, and his wife was obedient. Sure enough it was the disease the husband discovered, and she received treatment which probably saved the life of both the mother and child.

over a child. She is his equal, not his inferior. Therefore, a husband must respect her dignity in this regard both as to the matters and manner in which he exercises his authority. Because the wife, as the bearer and principal caretaker of small children, must first of all attend to the internal ordering of the household, typically, deference should be given to the wife's decisions and desires regarding these internal household matters (for example, how the home is to be organized and decorated, the chores the children should be assigned, etc.). Moreover, the husband should restrict the exercise of his authority to those areas which truly pertain to the common good of the marriage and family, not for the sake of his own private advantage.

INDISSOLUBILITY OF MARRIAGE

Another property of marriage as a consequence of its sacramental meaning is that in marriage one man and one woman are inseparably united to signify that Christ is faithful and inseparably united to only one Church.[36] St. Thomas teaches that among the goods of marriage, the sacramental sign is the greatest (even greater than the good of children), since it communicates grace.[37] He also teaches that the primary theological reason for the inseparability of sacramental matrimony is because it signifies the inseparable union of Christ and his Church:

> Inseparability belongs to marriage both insofar as it is a sign of the perpetual union of Christ and the Church, and insofar as it is for the duty of nature ordained to the good of offspring, as was said. But since the separation of marriage is more directly repugnant to the signification [of the sacrament] than to the good of the offspring (to which it is repugnant from the things which follow it, as was said); the inseparability of marriage is

36 This doctrine was forcefully reasserted in the document *Dominus Jesus* issued by the Congregation for the Doctrine of the Faith on Aug. 6th, 2000.
37 *In IV Sent.*, d.31, q.1, a.3.

more understood in the good of the sacrament than in
the good of offspring, although in either one it can be
understood.[38]

Because of this indissolubility, each spouse is bound to remain
faithful regardless of the fidelity of the other. Marriage vows are not
made in the conditional form: "If you are faithful . . ." but rather are
made absolutely and categorically in order to reflect the unconditional love of Christ for the Church. Thus even if a spouse is abandoned through no fault of their own, they must remain faithful as
a sacrament of Christ's love.[39] Such great love requires risk of being
unloved in return, and may seem above the human mode, but Christ
himself has taken the risk of loving us in this way and will give the
power to love as he has, in accordance with his own commandment:
"love one another as I have loved you."[40]

When spouses fail to maintain fidelity, this leads to a failure in
faith about Christ and his Church. It is not surprising then that in
an age where many spouses divorce and remarry the teaching that
there is only one Church, outside of which there is no salvation, is
widely denied.

It is also not surprising that there is a movement to divorce the
sacramental meaning of marriage from the sacramental meaning of
reception of the Eucharist (for example, by permitting the divorced
and remarried to receive sacramental communion). The truth, however, is that the Sacraments of Matrimony and the Eucharist are
inseparably united. Just as the natural order is unified and inter-
nally harmonious, so too is the sacramental order. Through sacramental communion, Christ gives himself in an act of spousal love
and fidelity to his Church.[41] But when someone has broken their
marriage bond, they are signifying by that act that Christ and the

---

38   *In IV Sent.*, d.33, q.2, a.1, ad.2.

39   Cf. 2 Tim. 2:13.

40   Jn 13:34 (NAB).

41   Pope Francis underlines this in *Evangelium Gaudii* when he asserts
that the priesthood is "a sign of Christ the Spouse who gives himself in the
Eucharist" (EG 104).

Church are no longer united and are not faithful to one another.[42] So it is this same spousal love and fidelity signified in the Eucharist which is objectively and sacramentally denied when spouses break their marriage bond and enter into a new union. And just as the conjugal act is forbidden when two persons are not indissolubly united in marriage, so also sacramental communion is forbidden to those who deny in their actions that Christ is indissolubly united with his Church. So the Church's discipline forbidding sacramental communion to those who have not been faithful to their marriage is not only because they are in an objectively sinful state. This is a general reason for forbidding communion applicable to any case of serious sin. But the specific and proper reason why the Church forbids sacramental communion to those who have not been faithful to their marriage is because it involves a denial at the sacramental and supernatural level of the very thing which sacramental communion affirms: the union of spousal charity.[43] Cardinal Müller, the former prefect for the Congregation for the Doctrine of the faith, asserts this same teaching:

> The basic principle is that no one can truly desire a Sacrament, that of the Eucharist, without also desiring to live in accord with the other Sacraments, including that of Marriage. One who lives in contrast with the

42 "The Church reaffirms her practice, which is based upon Sacred Scripture, of not admitting to Eucharistic Communion divorced persons who have remarried. They are unable to be admitted thereto from the fact that their state and condition of life objectively contradict that union of love between Christ and the Church which is signified and effected by the Eucharist." *Familiaris Consortio* 84.

43 Notice that it is the dissolution of the union which results in the prohibition of communion, not only the actual attempt to remarry. Thus, the same prohibition would exist for someone who separated from his spouse and publicly declared their intention to remarry, or who is sexually intimate with someone other than their spouse, even though not civilly remarried. On the other hand, mere physical separation does not signify the breaking of the marriage bond, so long as each spouse intends to remain faithful to the other. Marriage is not directly a promise to live together, but rather is a promise to give to someone the exclusive right over their bodies for acts apt to generate children.

marriage bond is opposed to the visible sign of the Sacrament of Marriage. In that which touches his bodily existence, even if he should be subjectively not culpable, he makes himself an "anti-sign" of indissolubility. And precisely because his bodily life is contrary to the sign, he cannot be part, in receiving communion, of the supreme Eucharistic sign, where the incarnate love of Jesus is revealed. The Church, if she were to admit this, would fall into what Saint Thomas Aquinas called "falsity in sacramental signs."[44]

To allow a sacramental practice which at once denies and affirms Christ's fidelity and charity for his Spouse is to destroy the unity and meaning of the sacramental order. Thus, reception of communion by the divorced and remarried harms not just the individuals involved by the unworthy reception of communion, but it harms the common good of the whole Church since this denial of the sacramental order distorts the meaning and unity of the sacraments and so, for the whole community, destroys the possibility of knowing and entering into the heavenly realities in which mankind finds salvation.

Notice also that the question of the subjective moral culpability of the person is not the determining consideration here. The denial of the sacramental order is made at the objective level, not merely the subjective level.[45] If someone outwardly indicated they intended

44   Speech at the Metropolitan Seminary of Oviedo in Spain. The English translation can be found at: http://chiesa.espresso.repubblica.it/articolo/1351294bdc4.html?eng=y. Instances where St. Thomas mentions a falsity in the sacred signs include: *S. T.*, IIIa, q.68, a.4; *S. T.*, IIIa, q.80, a.4; and Commentary on 1 Cor., c.11, lec.7.

45   St. Thomas Aquinas carefully distinguishes between judgments of conscience made in the private forum and judgments of conscience made in the public and objective forum. Responding to an objection that a judge must use his private knowledge (unknown to others) in a public proceeding in order to be faithful to his own conscience, St. Thomas replies: "A man in those things which pertain to his private person ought to inform his conscience from his private knowledge. But in those things which pertain to public power, he ought to inform his conscience according to those things which are able to be known in public judgment," (*S. T.*, II-IIae, q.67, a.2, ad.4). St. Thomas is so insistent

to persevere in a sinful life, they would not be a candidate for baptism or even absolution. This is true even if inwardly they intended to repent.[46] Similarly, a candidate for priestly ordination might inwardly believe in the teachings of the Church, but for whatever reason he might insist on using words which outwardly and objectively deny those teachings. This objective denial of the teachings of the Church would be a reason for not admitting such a person to Holy Orders in the Church.[47] Along the same lines, Cardinal Müller also says that the attempt to discern between those who are subjectively guilty and those who are not for purposes of receiving communion is not possible:

> This discernment would ultimately be impossible because only God examines hearts. Moreover, the economy of the Sacraments is an economy of visible signs, not of internal dispositions or subjective culpability. A privatization of the Sacramental economy would certainly not be Catholic. This is not a matter of discerning a mere interior

that this is necessary for the common good that he says even if a judge has to pronounce a death sentence to a man he privately knows is innocent, he should do so if the public evidence for his guilt is sufficient, and there is no way to publicly manifest his innocence (see *S. T.*, II-IIae, q.64, a.6, ad.3). Similarly, in order to safeguard the common good of the Church, a priest ought to deny public communion to those whom he knows are not guilty, but who outwardly appear guilty of adultery or other outwardly manifest grave sins. Conversely, if a priest knows by private knowledge (for example, from the confessional) that someone is guilty of a serious sin, yet there is no public evidence for this, he should not publicly deny communion to such a person based solely on his private knowledge. For more detailed defense of this teaching, see: "The Formation and Exercise of Conscience in Private and Public Matters," Sebastian Walshe, O.Praem., *Nova et Vetera*, Vol. 16, no.1, (winter 2018).

46   In a similar context, St. Thomas teaches: "In the sacramental signs there ought not to be some falsity. But a sign is false if it does not correspond to the thing signified. But from the fact that someone presents himself to be washed through Baptism, it is signified that he has disposed himself for interior cleansing, which does not happen to one who has the intention of persisting in sin." (*S. T.*, IIIa, q.68, a.4, c.).

47   Indeed, it would be a reason for not admitting someone to visible membership in the Church in the case of a catechumen.

disposition, but rather, as St. Paul says, of "discerning the body" (cf. *Amoris Laetitia* 185-186), the concrete visible relations in which we live.[48]

The Church is not merely an invisible union of souls known to God alone, but a visible sign: a sacrament. A sacrament is by its very nature a visible sign, and it is this visible and public dimension of the Church which demands that the public celebration of the sacraments conform to their outward significance. Thus an instruction by the Congregation for the Doctrine of the Faith taught:

> Marriage, in fact, because it is both the image of the spousal relationship between Christ and His Church as well as the fundamental core and an important factor in the life of civil society, is essentially a public reality... Thus, the judgment of conscience of one's own marital situation does not regard only the immediate relationship between man and God, as if one could prescind from the Church's mediation, that also includes the canonical laws binding in conscience. Not to recognize this essential aspect would mean in fact to deny that marriage is a reality of the Church, that is to say, a sacrament.[49]

There are, in sum, three reasons why someone cannot be admitted to sacramental communion if they are divorced and civilly remarried: 1) *Those aware that they are in mortal sin cannot receive the Eucharist without committing sacrilege.* As St. Paul says: "For anyone who eats and drinks without discerning the body, eats and drinks judgment on himself."[50] 2) *Even those who, with good reason,*

48   Speech at the Metropolitan Seminary of Oviedo in Spain. The English translation can be found at: http://chiesa.espresso.repubblica.it/articolo/1351294bdc4.html?eng=y.

49   Congregation for the Doctrine of the Faith: *Communion for the Divorced and Remarried Members of the Faithful*, Sept. 14, 1994, nn.7-8.

50   1 Cor 11:29 (NAB).

consider themselves subjectively not guilty of mortal sin ought to prefer the common good of the Church over their own private good. For
when there is no way to publicly manifest someone's innocence,
admitting them to communion would have the same effect on the
common good as admitting those who are in fact guilty.[51] Nor could
any reason be given for not admitting to sacramental communion
everyone who seems manifestly guilty of grave sin. 3) *The very
meaning of the Sacraments of Matrimony and the Eucharist would
be destroyed by the public admission of those who outwardly are guilty
of infidelity.* For the sacramental order is an order of visible signs, not
interior dispositions. We were not saved by an invisible God in an
invisible Church, but by an Incarnate God through a visible Church.

It is very important to understand however, that the prohibition
of sacramental communion for divorced and remarried Catholics
is not an assertion that the Church no longer cares for them, even
those who are guilty through their own choices. To the contrary,
just as a loving mother shows her care for her disobedient children by disciplining them, so too the Church shows her love for
her wayward children by discipline. A mother who punishes her
children does not want them to leave the family, but rather wants
them to leave behind the things which have caused them to distance
themselves from the family. So too, the denial of sacramental communion is not the Church rejecting her children, but the Church
calling her children to penance: to reject the very things by which
they have separated themselves from the family of God. Those who,
contrary to the command of Christ, have broken their marriage
bond and entered into a new marriage have made a decision to
love someone contrary to the will of Jesus. But as Jesus said: "If
any one comes to me without hating his father and mother, wife
and children, brothers and sisters, and even his own life, he cannot
be my disciple."[52] This does not mean that we want evil for our

51   There may be the possibility, however, of privately admitting someone
to communion whose innocence is demonstrable in the internal forum (for
example, if a divorced and remarried couple having small children are living
as brother and sister for the sake of raising their children).

52   Lk 14:26 (NAB).

family or ourselves, but it does mean that if we are forced to choose between Christ and some family member, we should choose as if we love Christ and hate all others. Those who have chosen divorce and remarriage have chosen to prefer their new spouse to Christ. But God did not make us for any human person, he has made us for himself! And any attempt to find happiness in someone other than Christ is doomed to fail. Therefore, the Church, ever solicitous for the true well-being of her children, calls them to repentance and full communion. Mercy for Jesus means opening up the possibility of reunion with God. It never means accepting or encouraging the things which keep us from union with God. Persons who have broken faith with their spouse should be helped to convert, not deceived into thinking that their situation is pleasing to God. Therefore, to the extent that they are able, divorced and remarried Catholics should participate in the life of the Church and seek through prayer, penance and the loving attention of the community, the grace to be fully reunited to Christ.[53]

As for those who, through no fault of which they are conscious, find themselves in an objective situation which prohibits them from receiving communion, these must first of all remember the teaching of Scripture that "all the ways of a man may be pure in his own eyes, but it is the Lord who proves the spirit."[54] In other words, each one should have the humility to acknowledge that he is not the ultimate arbiter of the truth, even the truth about himself.[55] So one should recognize that if there is no way to manifest their innocence in a public, ecclesiastical forum, perhaps this is because they are misjudging their own situation.

53   "[The divorced and remarried] should be encouraged to listen to the word of God, to attend the Sacrifice of the Mass, to persevere in prayer, to contribute to works of charity and to community efforts in favor of justice, to bring up their children in the Christian faith, to cultivate the spirit and practice of penance and thus implore, day by day, God's grace. Let the Church pray for them, encourage them and show herself a merciful mother, and thus sustain them in faith and hope." *Familiaris Consortio*, 84.

54   Prov 16:2 (NAB), cf. Prov 21:2 and 20:24.

55   See 1 Cor. 4:4 (NAB): "I am not conscious of anything against me, but I do not thereby stand acquitted; the one who judges me is the Lord."

Even in the case where one is convinced and certain of their own innocence in the internal forum, assisted by the judgment of a confessor, he must consider first and foremost the will of God and the common good before his private good. It sometimes happens that without their fault, God permits his faithful servants to be deprived of certain goods for which they might otherwise have a just claim. For example, a man or woman may be abandoned by their spouse without a just reason, and so are unjustly deprived of the comforts and use of marriage. Their vow and the common good demands that such persons refrain from seeking the goods of marriage from another. And while this entails a great sacrifice, it would entail the loss of a greater good if they were to seek remarriage. For the common good is truly *their* personal good, not an alien good; and it is an even greater good than their private good.[56] For example, if abandonment by a spouse were accepted as a sufficient reason to remarry, this would require that marriage vows are merely conditional: "If you are faithful to me, I will be faithful to you." Such a conditional love would destroy the true meaning of marital love, and reduce every marriage to a kind of contract rather than a communion established by a covenant. It is true: unconditional love expressed by unconditioned vows involves a risk, but it is a greater

---

56 See chapter 3 above, on the preferability of the common good over the private good. The Scriptures often testify to this truth and give many examples in which someone who is guilty of no fault still chooses to submit himself to a penalty or prescript of law for the sake of the common good. First of all, the Lord Jesus submitted himself to both the divine and human law though he was exempt. He submitted himself to the divine law upon coming into the world, as St. Paul teaches (Gal. 4:4), and in his death (Philip. 2:8). He submitted himself to human law when he accepted the sentence of Pontius Pilate (Jn. 19:11) and chose to pay the temple tax though he was exempt (Matt. 17:24-27) to avoid scandal. The Mother of the Lord also submitted herself to the common divine law, though she was exempt (Lk. 2:22). St. Paul enjoined the Romans to abstain from eating meat sacrificed to idols to avoid scandal (Rom. 14:13-15:1) and had Timothy undergo circumcision for the sake of avoiding scandal (Acts 16:3). Even reason without the light of faith can see this truth as Socrates willingly accepted the unjust sentence of death for the sake of respecting the laws of the state (*Crito*, 50a-b). All of these sacrificed their own private privileges for the sake of a higher good.

good for everyone that such a love is what is expected in every sacramental marriage. Similarly, it may happen that a faithful Catholic is deprived of the Eucharist through no fault of their own (for example, if they have been unjustly excommunicated). In such cases, they should not seek to receive the Eucharist by illicit means. Rather, they should offer this as a pleasing sacrifice to God for the sake of the common good which they still share with the whole Church. Indeed a spiritual communion made in such circumstances can be even more meritorious than a sacramental communion, since God sees not merely the outward reception of a sacrament, but also the great desire of the heart both for the Eucharist and to do God's will as manifested by the objective circumstances of one's life. Indeed, at every Mass immediately before the distribution of communion, we use the words of the centurion to profess our faith in the power of a spiritual communion: "Lord, I am not worthy that you should enter under my roof, but only say the word and my soul shall be healed." Just as the servant of the centurion was healed without Jesus' physical presence, so too the soul can be healed without Jesus coming sacramentally. Pope-emeritus Benedict XVI has spoken beautifully and compassionately of this in his book *Behold the Pierced One*,[57] written while he was a cardinal.

In a passage particularly apt to the question at hand, the Second Book of Maccabees records that Eleazar was offered the opportunity to eat meat which was according to the law, yet which to others appeared contrary to the law:

> Those in charge of that unlawful ritual meal took the man aside privately, because of their long acquaintance with him, and urged him to bring meat of his own providing, such as he could legitimately eat, and to pretend to be eating some of the meat of the sacrifice prescribed by the king; in this way he would escape the death penalty, and be treated kindly because of their old friendship with him. But he made up his mind in

57   Published by Ignatius Press, 1984.

a noble manner, worthy of his years, the dignity of his advanced age, the merited distinction of his gray hair, and of the admirable life he had lived from childhood; and so he declared that above all he would be loyal to the holy laws given by God. He told them to send him at once to the abode of the dead, explaining: "At our age it would be unbecoming to make such a pretense; many young men would think the ninety-year-old Eleazar had gone over to an alien religion. Should I thus dissimulate for the sake of a brief moment of life, they would be led astray by me."[58]

Subjectively in his conscience Eleazar knew that the meat could be eaten without contravening God's law, but because this was not public knowledge, his conscience instructed him that a higher law was to be followed for the sake of the common good. Similarly, those who in their conscience believe that it is licit for them to receive communion also must meet the demands of their conscience for the preservation of the good of the Church and the sacramental order.

MARRIAGE IS A COMMUNION

Another consequence of the sacramental meaning of marriage is that the spouses are called to communion, that is, to the sharing of one life. For as Christ communicates his own life (i.e., sanctifying grace, which especially comes through the Eucharist) to the Church, so also a husband and wife ought to share in one life. This union of lives obviously requires openness between spouses. Jesus called his disciples "friends" because he had revealed to them everything he had heard from his Father.[59] Spouses too should have no secrets from one another, but should communicate and share openly all that is of importance to one another. Sharing a life also requires the sacrifices involved in spending time together. For example, the husband should not spend unnecessary time at work or with friends

58   2 Macc 6:21-25 (NAB).
59   Cf., Jn 15:15.

away from his family. It is interesting to note that it was precisely when Adam was away from his wife Eve that the serpent found an opportunity to tempt her. Had they been together, perhaps they might have been able to resist his temptations.

So powerful is the sacramental meaning of communion in marriage that St. Paul appeals to this aspect of marriage as an argument against fornication:

> Do you not know that your bodies are members of Christ? Shall I then take Christ's members and make them the members of a prostitute? Of course not! Or do you not know that anyone who joins himself to a prostitute becomes one body with her? For 'the two,' it says, 'will become one flesh.' But whoever is joined to the Lord becomes one spirit with him. Avoid immorality. Every other sin a person commits is outside the body, but the immoral person sins against his own body. Do you not know that your body is a temple of the Holy Spirit within you, whom you have from God, and that you are not your own?[60]

St. Paul asserts that in the union of Christ and his Church, "whoever is joined to the Lord becomes one spirit with him." This means that they share the same life principle, and hence the same life. And from this he argues that fornication brings Christ into union with a prostitute through the body of the believer. True, fornication is wrong because it is an unreasonable use of the reproductive power since children are meant to be raised by parents in a stable union. Yet, St. Paul gives a more powerful argument why the faithful ought not to engage in fornication. And this argument is based upon the sacramental meaning of marriage as a sign of the union of Christ and his Church. Revealed truth gives a more profound perspective on the meaning and purpose of human sexuality. As C.S. Lewis put it:

60 1 Cor 6:16-19 (NAB).

One of the ends for which sex was created was to symbolize to us the hidden things of God. One of the functions of human marriage is to express the nature of the union between Christ and the Church. We have no authority to take the living and sensitive figures which God has painted on the canvas of our nature and shift them about as if they were mere geometrical figures ... we are dealing with male and female not merely as facts of nature but as the live and awful shadows of realities utterly beyond our control and largely beyond our direct knowledge. Or rather, we are not dealing with them but (as we shall soon learn if we meddle) they are dealing with us.[61]

MARRIAGE IS FOR THE SAKE OF BEGETTING NEW LIFE

Finally, from the fact that marriage is meant to signify the union of Christ and his Church, we can see the reason why marital intercourse ought to be done with love and should be, in itself, ordered to the begetting of new life. For the husband's act of love begetting children through and in his wife is for the sake of signifying the act of love by which Christ begets new faithful through and in his Church. The Church cooperates with Christ in the work of evangelization, catechesis and baptism by which new faithful are born; but the primary agent in all these works is Christ himself working through the Holy Spirit who is Love. Sexual intercourse carried out in a way which is not ordered to begetting new life would be like evangelizing, catechizing and baptizing in a way that is not ordered to spiritual rebirth. Or for a husband to have intercourse with his wife without love, but out of lust, would signify not the love of Christ, but rather self-interest. From this it is obvious why contraception or unnatural forms of sexual intercourse are wrong as distortions of the meaning of the sacrament of marriage.

---

61   *God in the Dock*, Part II, chapter 11: "Priestesses in the Church?"

THE PASCAL MYSTERY AS A SACRAMENT OF THE UNION OF CHRIST AND HIS CHURCH

Not only is the Incarnation itself signified by the Sacrament of Matrimony, but also the things which Christ suffered and did in his incarnate flesh are signified by the Sacrament of Matrimony. Every sacrament takes its power and meaning from the Passion and Resurrection of our Savior, Jesus Christ.[62] The Sacrament of Matrimony takes its origin and meaning from the Passion and Resurrection of Christ in a special way.[63] The early Fathers of the Church immediately recognized the likeness between the sleep of Christ on the Cross as water and blood flowed from his pierced side, and the sleep of Adam as God opened his side and formed for him a Bride.[64] Through the sacraments of Baptism and the Eucharist, symbolized by the flowing water and blood, the Church, the Bride of Christ, was formed from the side of Christ. And so also in the Passion of the Lord we recognize the Sacrament of Matrimony.

St. Paul not only mentions that the union of husband and wife is a sign of the union of Christ and his Church, but also expressly connects the Sacrament of Matrimony with the Passion of the Lord:

> Wives should be subordinate to their husbands as to the Lord. For the husband is head of his wife just as Christ is head of the church, *he himself the savior* of the body. As the church is subordinate to Christ, so wives should be subordinate to their husbands in everything. Husbands, love your wives, *even as Christ loved the church*

---

62   Cf. *S. T.*, IIIa, q.62, a.5.

63   "In this sacrifice [of Christ for the Church] there is entirely revealed that plan which God imprinted on the humanity of man and woman since their creation." *Familiaris Consortio* 13; "By virtue of the mystery of the death and Resurrection of Christ, of which the spouses are made part in a new way by marriage, conjugal love is purified and made holy." *Familiaris Consortio* 56.

64   The *Catechism of the Catholic Church* quotes St. Ambrose: "As Eve was formed from the sleeping Adam's side, so the Church was born from the pierced heart of Christ hanging dead on the cross." (CCC n.766). See also, for example, Quodvultdeus, *Book of Promises and Predictions of God*, 1, 3; St. Augustine, *City of God*, 22, 17; and St. John Chrysostom, *Catecheses*, 3, 13-19.

and handed himself over for her to sanctify her, cleansing
her by the bath of water with the word, that he might
present to himself the church in splendor, without spot
or wrinkle or any such thing, that she might be holy
and without blemish. So (also) husbands should love
their wives as their own bodies. He who loves his wife
loves himself. For no one hates his own flesh but rather
nourishes and cherishes it, even as Christ does the
church, because we are members of his body. 'For this
reason a man shall leave (his) father and (his) mother
and be joined to his wife, and the two shall become one
flesh.' This is a great mystery, but I speak in reference to
Christ and the church.[65]

The Lord has left every husband an example of how to love his
wife and how he ought to show this love. A husband is to sacrifice
himself and the desires of his flesh in order to sanctify her, leading
her to Christ especially through the sacraments and pondering over
the word of God together.

A husband is in a special way conformed to Christ crucified. But
far from being a cause of sorrow, this is a cause of joy. True love,
pure and intense, longs to show the beloved its full measure. The
soul of the lover is restless and dissatisfied so long as the beloved
does not know the entirety of his love for her. This longing is like
an agony of the heart if there is no outlet by which the intensity of
its love might be unbound. Self-sacrifice is precisely this outlet of
love. The Lord expresses this suffering longing when he exclaimed:
"I have come to set the earth on fire, and how I wish it were already
blazing! There is a baptism with which I must be baptized, and how
great is my anguish until it is accomplished!"[66] And so the lover
prefers hardship and suffering in the body so that the soul might be
freed from the anguish of a love unseen by its beloved. The desire
for union in marriage should include a desire to sacrifice oneself for

65   Eph 5:22-32 (NAB) (emphasis mine).
66   Lk 12:49-50 (NAB).

the beloved, so that the Passion of Christ might be more fully and perfectly signified and manifested in marriage.

But it is not only the Passion which reveals the mystery of marriage. The Resurrection of the Lord also reveals profound truths about the union between a husband and his wife. This is why the Lord so often compares Heaven to an eternal wedding banquet. On the Cross, our Savior handed himself over to death for his Bride, and as a consequence, he was for a time separated from her. By the Resurrection, Christ and his Church are reunited in a more profound way than they had been before the Passion. Now that the Church understands the depth of Christ's love, the joy of their union is unassailable, and the union itself indissoluble. So also, together with the sacrifices of marriage, there are the profound joys which can come only after love has been manifested through sacrifice. In these times the spouses are a sign of the Resurrection of the Lord and the eternal joy which is the destiny of all who take up their cross and follow Christ.

OBJECTIONS AND ANSWERS

Objection 1: There are many ways in which marriage is not like the Incarnation. For example, married people are two different substances not one, and man and woman are the same nature, while humanity and divinity are not. Moreover, there are many ways in which marriage is not like the union of Christ and the Church. For example, the Church is not a person, but a wife is a person. Therefore, marriage is not an apt sign of these supernatural realities.

Answer: As mentioned above, a sign is that which strikes the senses and calls to mind something other than itself. Therefore, what is required for an apt sign is that it in some way be better known than the thing signified and that it somehow be associated with the thing signified. For one thing to be associated with another thing it is not required that they be alike in every respect. (Indeed, it is not required that there be a likeness at all. For example, most words do not sound like the thing they signify, but are only associated with them by our memory of hearing those sounds in the presence of the things they signify). If the sign and the thing signified were alike in every respect, the sign would cease to be a sign. Therefore, it is sufficient that there be some association between marriage and the Incarnation, and marriage and the union of Christ and his Church. This association is established through: 1) the revelation that God intends to signify the union of Christ and the Church and the Incarnation through the Sacrament of Matrimony; and 2) the many likenesses which marriage has to these mysteries of the faith.

Objection 2: Since marriage is not like the Incarnation or the union of Christ and the Church in every respect, then it follows that marriage is not a necessary sign for understanding these things after all. For we understand the aspects of the Incarnation and the union of Christ and the Church which are not signified by marriage (for example, we understand that the divinity and humanity in Christ are united in a single person not merely in a moral union). Therefore, different understandings of marriage will have no effect upon our understanding of the other aspects of these mysteries.

Answer: Something can be necessary in two ways. In one way, something is necessary for the being of another thing. For example, sides are necessary if a triangle is to exist. In another way, something is necessary for the well-being of a thing. For example, an education is necessary for the well-being of a child. Marriage is a sign which is necessary in order that we understand well the mysteries of the Incarnation and the union of Christ and his Church. Indeed, the fact that God has chosen to use the sign of marriage to signify the union of the divine and the human indicates that it is an especially helpful sign, and necessary for a perfect understanding of these mysteries. Moreover, since God has established that marriage should be a sign of these mysteries, any distortion of the meaning of marriage will necessarily lead one astray who attempts to approach these mysteries through their distorted understanding of marriage.

Objection 3: But if marriage need not be like the Incarnation or the union of Christ and the Church in every respect, can someone just arbitrarily look for what they think are likenesses and then draw whatever conclusions they want about marriage and family life, or conversely, about the Incarnation or the union of Christ and the Church? For example, since the divine nature is of infinitely greater dignity than human nature, and the divine nature is signified by the husband, while the human nature is signified by the wife, the husband should be considered to have infinitely greater dignity than his wife.

Answer: A sign and the thing signified are not related in such a way that the whole understanding of one is contained in the other and vice-versa (as happens, for example, in the relationship between double and half). So our understanding of the union of the human and divine does not depend entirely upon our understanding of marriage. Nor does our understanding of marriage depend entirely upon an understanding of the union of the human and divine. For example, the analogy of the union of soul and body is an apt sign for understanding the union of the divine and human in the Incarnation, and the concepts of man and God can also lead us to an understanding of the Incarnation. Therefore, the fact that there are ways in which marriage is unlike the Incarnation and unlike the union of Christ and his Church do not necessarily lead one into error. Yet the fact that God has identified marriage as a sign of the union of the divine and human means that marriage is a privileged means of coming to know these mysteries better. Given the fact of divine revelation, the duty of the believer is to discover as many likenesses as he can for the sake of more deeply understanding that revelation. Moreover, this kind of knowledge is less abstract and more akin to experiential knowledge: the person who has been in a holy marriage, or who at least has witnessed one, has an experience that is like these mysteries which no other experience can give. Therefore, the fact that there are other means of knowing the Incarnation and the union of Christ and his Church does not make marriage dispensable as a sign of these things.

8

The Holy Family as Source of Revelation

IN ALL LIVING THINGS, THE FUNDAMENTAL
building block is the cell, in which the whole is somehow recapit-
ulated or existent in seminal form. Something like this can be said
about the family in relation to the whole Church. John Paul II used
to refer to the family as the "domestic church."

THE HOLY FAMILY:

Nowhere is the Church found more powerfully in domestic form
than in the Holy Family. In that pristine society and communion,
the Son of God and his mother lived under the care of St. Joseph.
The principal members of the Church were all together in one
family. The communion among the Persons of the Trinity and the
sharing of life between the divine and human natures in Christ
are also reflected most perfectly in the Holy Family. For example,
we have already seen evidence of the perfect communion which
existed within the Holy Family. St. Joseph exhibited the love "which
believes all things" when he took Mary into his home though she
was found to be with child. Mary in her turn manifested her trust
in Joseph's care by obeying his word that they had to flee to Egypt.
Between the parents and the child Jesus, there also existed an open
and complete sharing of life and goods. It was a sharing which
began even before the birth of the child, for in view of his foreseen
merits, Mary was preserved free from all stain of original sin. And
we can reasonably infer that the singular graces given to St. Joseph
were also in preparation for his mission as spouse of the Mother
of God and head of the Holy Family.

When God became man, he could have assumed our nature in any number of possible ways. He could have come as a full-grown man, like Adam, without human generation. He could have been born of a virgin who was not married. But instead, he desired to assume our nature as part of a complete human family, with both father and mother. This simple fact of revelation already manifests a profound truth: the natural human family is the ideal place for a child to come to be and to live. With all his wisdom and omnipotence, God could find no better place in which to be born and live. Attempts by modern man to find a better substitute for the natural family are destined to fail.

Another consequence of God's choice to come into the world in this way is that, from all eternity, the Person of God the Son saw himself as a member of a human family. It is the same Person who is God and man. That divine Person, from the perspective of eternity, in which all times are equally present to him, always saw and considered himself to be a member of a human family. For him, the Incarnation was not something in the future, it was something always present to him, and always part of his personality. This means that, from God's viewpoint, the human family is not simply an afterthought, or a mere vehicle for multiplying the human race. The human family was something present to the mind of God from all eternity as pertaining to his very identity and mission. Therefore, the human family transcends the created order in its dignity and nobility. St. Thomas says something like this in referring to the dignity of the Virgin Mary: "The blessed Virgin, from the fact that she is the mother of God, has a certain infinite dignity from the infinite good which is God."[1]

God's choice in establishing and governing the Holy Family manifests another truth about the human family, namely that the relationships within a family are not simply a matter of necessity or competence to carry out a function. This truth is especially striking in the case of the Holy Family. If ever a father and husband were unnecessary and expendable in a family from the perspective of

---

1   *S. T.*, Ia, q.25, a.6, ad.4. Cf., *In III Sent.* d.44, q.1, a.3, c.

functionality, it was in the Holy Family. St. Joseph was not necessary to beget or even educate the child. God was the child's Father and the Holy Spirit was the Spouse of the Virgin Mary. St. Joseph was not necessary as a moral or intellectual guide to his spouse who was conceived without original sin, and is acclaimed by the Church as Virgin Most Prudent, and Seat of Wisdom. The power of miracles or angelic protection could have sufficed to provide and protect the child and his mother. Yet in spite of all this, God willed the Holy Family to have a husband and father, and it was through St. Joseph that he guided the Holy Family in the early years of the life of Jesus. In the one case where God could have done without a husband and father, he chose not to. To the contrary, Scripture asserts that St. Joseph's presence in the Holy Family is essential and even enjoys a certain primacy. Consider the passage from the opening chapter of St. Matthew's Gospel:

> Now this is how the birth of Jesus Christ came about. When his mother Mary was betrothed to Joseph, but before they lived together, she was found with child through the Holy Spirit. Joseph her husband, since he was a righteous man, yet unwilling to expose her to shame, decided to divorce her quietly. Such was his intention when, behold, the angel of the Lord appeared to him in a dream and said, 'Joseph, son of David, do not be afraid to take Mary your wife into your home. For it is through the Holy Spirit that this child has been conceived in her. She will bear a son and you are to name him Jesus, because he will save his people from their sins.' All this took place to fulfill what the Lord had said through the prophet: 'Behold, the virgin shall be with child and bear a son, and they shall name him Emmanuel,' which means 'God is with us.' When Joseph awoke, he did as the angel of the Lord had commanded him and took his wife into his home. He had no relations with her until she bore a son, and he named him Jesus.[2]

2   Matt 1:18-25 (NAB).

If someone were to ask you: "How did the birth of Jesus come about?" I suppose that most people would answer by relating the story of the angel's annunciation to Mary, and her consent, and subsequent journey to Bethlehem where Jesus was born in a stable. Probably most people would say that St. Joseph had little or no role to play in the birth of Jesus, yet when St. Matthew answers this question, his entire narrative focuses on St. Joseph and the choices he had to make. Joseph is the one to whom the angel appears. Joseph is the one who takes Mary into his home. Joseph is the one who names the child Jesus.

Again, when the life of the child Jesus was threatened by Herod, God did not act through the child or Mary, even though both were holier and wiser than Joseph. Instead, God lead the Holy Family through Joseph on three occasions. Consider too Mary's obedience. Her husband wakes up from a dream and tells her they are to leave in the middle of the night for Egypt; that they would have to travel dangerous roads by night filled with robbers and beasts with a new-born child; that they would have to go to a far-off land where they did not speak the language or have work. And she had just a short time to gather together some necessities and leave behind her home and family and friends without so much as a goodbye. Yet faced with this Mary does not argue. That is trust.

So even in the case of the Holy Family where from a functional point of view St. Joseph seems unnecessary and even superfluous, God wills that he be an essential member of that family. Grace builds upon, preserves and perfects nature, even in its most extraordinary manifestations. So obviously, from God's perspective, the persons and relationships within a family are not simply for the sake of carrying out traditional functions. They are also indispensable signs of higher realities.

Finally, the Son of God chose to come into a poor family which would be persecuted, and have to migrate to a foreign land. He did this first of all to teach us not to fear poverty or external hardships: there can be love and joy even in such circumstances so long as the spouses love and trust God and one another. God permits no evil except to bring from it a greater good. After all, what would

Christmas be if Jesus had been born in a hotel or a palace? God also entered a family in such circumstances to teach us not to despise the poor, the persecuted, the migrants and the foreigners. For his own family was once poor and dwelt in a foreign land.

PART III

*Practical Applications
to Families*

9

The Christian Family

IN THE THIRD AND FINAL PART OF THIS CON-
sideration of the Theology of the family, I will focus briefly upon
some practical applications of the foregoing principles, and will give
some concrete signs and recommendations for bringing about a
healthy, flourishing Christian family.

WHAT DOES THE FLOURISHING CHRISTIAN FAMILY LOOK LIKE?

Before considering the signs marking an ideal Christian family,
it might be helpful to indicate some things which might at first
look like signs of an ideal Christian family, but are not. For a Christian family to flourish, it is not necessary that there be no trials or
serious difficulties. Many trials such as financial failure, tragedies
from accidents, sickness, physical or mental disabilities, etc., not
only are not incompatible with a flourishing Christian family: they
are often key aspects which allow the supernatural character of a
flourishing Christian family to shine forth. Certain Christian virtues
simply cannot grow to perfection without serious trials and obstacles. Even the Holy Family experienced misunderstandings which
were unavoidable, as when St. Joseph did not understand how his
wife was with child (cf. Matt 1:19), and the parents of Jesus did not
understand why he had left without telling them (cf. Lk 2:48). These
misunderstandings became the occasion of great trust and the love
which "believes all things."[1] St. James says simply: "Consider it all
joy, my brothers, when you encounter various trials."[2] Having set

1   1 Cor 13:7 (NAB).
2   Jas 1:2 (NAB). Thus, a family in which one or more of the children suffer
from Downs Syndrome, for example, or a family in which a parent is or becomes

aside that misconception, what are some marks of a flourishing Christian family?

1ST MARK: INTEGRITY

The first mark of a flourishing Christian family is integrity, namely, that the whole family (i.e., father, mother and children) is present and active. The family is not divided by divorce, or strife between the parents or among the children. The family is often together as a whole on a daily basis. The father does not go off frequently on his own away from the family. The mother is not frequently away from her husband or her children. The children are not usually out with their friends apart from the rest of the family.

2ND MARK: COMMUNION

Communion, as we said above, means that the members within the family share one life. Each person in a happy family knows, loves, is known by, and is loved by all the others. Therefore there is a mutual containment of each in each, or of all in all, by love and knowledge. Moreover, in a family, it is possible for all the members to be united by ties of blood and generation — even the husband and wife share blood relations to their child. Again, in a family, the

---

handicapped, are often the families in which Christian virtues predominate. I still remember the sage advice one of my confreres gave me years ago. He said: "If you find out that a couple has had a child which is born with retardation or some serious physical handicap, do not tell them that you are sorry for them. Instead tell them to get down on their knees and thank God. Families who have such children, parents and siblings alike, inevitably grow much faster in Christian love." That observation has been true to my own experience, and I thought about why that is. At first I thought it was because everyone, parents and children alike, have to be responsible and care for their weaker family member. But later I realized that wasn't the most profound reason for the spiritual health of such families. The true reason is because the other children can see clearly in their sibling that their parent's love for them is not caused by their success according to some worldly standard, like intelligence, or good looks, or athleticism, or whatever. All the children in the family see clearly that their parents love them *because* they are their children. This gives them a deep security in their parent's love which ultimately leads them on to understand the divine love more perfectly. So the ideal Christian family is not one which may be ideal according to the world's standards.

members engage in daily activities together, such as common meals.

Within a family, the life of the father is in some sense lived by every other member, since the wife and children know and love and enjoy the life of the father (or sorrow with him). So too the life of the mother is in some sense lived by every other member, etc. So the family is not only a community, but also a communion of persons, at least to some extent, since all the members in some sense live the life of the father, and hence the family partakes of the unity of his individual life; and again, since all the members in some sense live the life of the mother, and hence the family partakes of the unity of her individual life, and so on with each child.

Communion between spouses is also reflected in marital intercourse which is open to the generation of new life. As shown above, self-movement and self-possession makes communion possible since nothing gives what it does not possess, and communion at its highest level involves giving oneself. For spouses to reflect and signify the mystery of Trinitarian communion, their mutual giving must be a giving of the totality of self: "The total physical self-giving [of intercourse] would be a lie if it were not the sign and fruit of total personal self-giving, in which the whole person, including the temporal dimension, is present."[3]

Last of all, communion implies openness and honesty among the members of a family. The spouses should have no secrets from each other. Jesus said that he called his disciples friends and not servants "because I have told you everything I have heard from my Father."[4] Likewise parents should be proactive in letting their children know that they want to know about their struggles and difficulties, and should make the children feel confident in their parent's help. This is especially true in matters pertaining to sexual morality, since the proper forum to learn about bringing new life into the world is within one's own family. Children on their part should be open with their parents especially when they find themselves confronted with temptations to sin. Fathers should be especially proactive in speaking to

3   *Familiaris Consortio* 11.
4   Jn 15:15 (NAB).

their sons, and mothers likewise with their daughters. Sons ought to learn how to be a man from their father, and girls ought to learn how to be a woman from their mother. Still, a certain reverence and modesty should be observed about the details of procreation even between parents and their children. Nature has equipped our species (as every species) with the instinctual knowledge of the details of procreation once the proper setting is in place. The instruction of the parents should focus primarily upon indicating what the proper setting is for marital intimacy, and the moral disposition with which to approach matters of sexual chastity. The parents should not primarily focus on the biological mechanics of reproduction.

3RD MARK: ORDER AND HARMONY

In a flourishing Christian family, there is order and harmony. We have already addressed this in some detail above in chapter 7. In summary, the love of the husband for his wife leaves no doubt that he exercises his authority for her good, and that he respects her as an equal, not as if she were one of the children. Moreover, the love of the parents for the children leave no doubt that they exercise their authority over their children for their good. The wife for her part respects and supports her husband, especially in difficult circumstances. The children give honor and cheerful obedience to their parents.[5] As a consequence, the family is able to act together as one, and work in harmony with one another. Each member of the family prefers the common good of the family to their private interests.

4TH MARK: BEGETTING NEW LIFE

The good is diffusive of itself. In other words, goodness draws and incorporates others into its own goodness. The happy family

---

5   Pope John Paul II identifies a mistaken concept of this order within a family as one of the root causes of disharmony within a family: "Signs are not lacking of a disturbing degradation of some fundamental values: a mistaken theoretical and practical concept of the independence of the spouses in relation to each other; serious misconceptions regarding the relationship of authority between parents and children..." *Familiaris Consortio* 6.

will diffuse its own goodness in the same way and will reflect more profoundly the generative aspect of communion found in God. A happily married couple who live in a communion of love will be generous in bringing new life into the world and communicating their own happiness to their children.[6] This communication of goodness and life to the children is the main business of Christian education, for the life of man is primarily the life of the spirit. It is also a sign for the children of the very love of God for them[7] as well as the love found in the Trinity of the Father for the Son.

Not only do the parents communicate goodness and life to their own children, the family as a whole communicates these gifts to those around them.[8] How attractive is a truly happy family life. The flourishing Christian family is not closed in on itself, but rather looks outward to bring the gifts of the Spirit to their neighbors and friends.[9] Generosity and hospitality are hallmarks of such a family.

For couples who are unable to have their own children or to adopt, this latter form of sharing goodness and life is especially predominant, since such couples are freer to share their time and resources with those outside their family.[10]

6   Plato argues for the intrinsic connection between love and procreation: "[Love] is a longing not for the beautiful itself, but for the conception and generation that the beautiful effects." *Symposium*, 206e.

7   "Parental love is called to become for the children the visible sign of the very love of God." *Familiaris Consortio* 14.

8   "The fruitfulness of conjugal love is not restricted solely to the procreation of children . . . it is enlarged and enriched by all those fruits of moral, spiritual and supernatural life which the father and mother are called to hand on to their children, and through the children to the Church and to the world." *Familiaris Consortio* 28.

9   As we shall see below, this trait of a flourishing Christian family will be an essential instrument for bringing about healing in families which suffer from serious defects.

10   "Physical sterility in fact can be for spouses the occasion for other important services to the life of the human person, for example, adoption, various forms of educational work, and assistance to other families and to poor and handicapped children." *Familiaris Consortio* 14.

5TH MARK: STRIVING BEYOND THE
NATURAL TO THE SUPERNATURAL

The most proper mark of a flourishing Christian family is that the supernatural goods are preeminent in such a way as to complete and perfect the natural goods of family life.

Sometimes one finds Catholic families in which the truths of the Faith hold first place in the lives of the parents and children, but in such a way that the natural goods are ignored or even looked upon with suspicion. The family attends daily Mass, the children are all perfectly dressed and well-behaved. But there is no genuine affection in the household between the husband and wife or between the parents and the children. For example, the father or mother might have a drinking problem; and fear, rather than joy, is the predominant emotion among the children. They fear their parents; they fear God; they fear the world. Such a household is more likely to produce animosity towards the truths of the Faith in the long run, since the children will associate those truths and practices with negative and painful emotions. The goods of nature and of grace both come from the hands of the good God, and grace is meant to build upon and perfect nature, not destroy it.

On the other hand, sometimes one finds Catholic families in which the natural goods are emphasized while the supernatural goods are marginalized, or treated as mere "icing on the cake." Prayer and the sacraments are seen as accessories but not necessary elements of a truly happy family life. Given the opportunity to go to daily Mass together as a family on the one hand or spending a leisurely breakfast at home on the other hand; or given the choice of watching a movie together instead of saying a family Rosary together, the choice is rarely for the supernatural good. Such a family prefers to live by sight not by faith. Both the family who disdains natural goods, and the family which ignores supernatural goods miss the mark of a truly flourishing Christian family.

This most proper mark of a flourishing Christian family should be evident in all the other marks listed above. The integrity and unity of the family finds its primary motive not in natural benefits, but in the fact that it is a living witness and sign of the integrity and unity of the life of the Trinity. The communion and openness among the members of the family is consciously intended to reflect the perfect communion among the three Persons of the Trinity. Spouses are aware that their relationship reflects the relationship between Christ and his Church. Parents see clearly in their love for their children a reflection of the Father's love for themselves. The goods which the parents communicate to their children and to others outside their homes are primarily spiritual goods: the truths of the faith, the love of prayer and the sacraments, etc. The entire life of the flourishing Christian family should be suffused with the supernatural: with faith, hope and charity, in such a way that the natural goods are perfected, not corrupted.

CONSECRATED LIFE AS A POINT OF REFERENCE FOR FAMILY LIFE

The family that exhibits these marks will quite naturally be fertile soil for vocations to consecrated life. Furthermore, the family itself will, in some way, strive to share in the goods attained through the evangelical counsels. John Paul II said that "the monastic experience constitutes the heart of Christian life, so much so that it can be proposed as a point of reference for all the baptized."[11] Monastic life is essentially a life given wholly and completely to God. It typically takes the form of three vows or promises made to God which dedicate the whole person to God: the vow of poverty by which all one's external possessions are given over to God; the vow of chastity, by which the goods of the body are given over to God; and the vow of obedience, by which the goods of the soul are given over to God. In some way the vows of poverty, chastity, and obedience will find expression in a happy Christian family. Detachment from wealth, and perhaps even times of actual poverty, will arise naturally from a preference for spiritual goods such as the virtue of generosity. A love for communion with God in prayer will moderate the desires of the flesh for procreation. The desire to serve one

11   Address of the Holy Father, Pope John Paul II, to the Congregation of the Holy Ghost, May 25th, 2002.

another will express itself in humble mutual subordination. And as spouses advance in age, as the duty of generating and educating children becomes less urgent and necessary, their life together should look more and more like the life of a brother and sister in a religious community, with their common interactions being more and more directly related to the love, service and praise of God.

10

Formation for Family Life

THE FAMILY IN ITS
SEMINAL STAGES

I HAVE CONSIDERED WHAT THE IDEAL CHRIS-
tian family should look like in its perfect form. This constitutes a
kind of target at which to aim when persons intend to bring such
a family into being. I will now consider the coming to be of the
Christian family, beginning with the formation of children for family life, followed by a consideration of dating and engagement, and
concluding with a treatment of newly married couples.

RAISING CHILDREN FOR FAMILY LIFE:
"Since parents have conferred life on their children, they have
a most solemn obligation to educate their offspring."[1] This right
and duty of parents cannot be completely delegated to or usurped
by others.[2]

Children should be raised in such a way that they are
well-suited for a happy family life. This means inculcating and
modeling the virtues which a good husband and father, wife and
mother ought to have when starting their own family. The primary
means by which these virtues are communicated to children is by
example. Words will do little or nothing if not exemplified by the
life of the parents.

Children must first of all see that the primary love and the primary relationship of communion within a family is between their

---

1   *Familiaris Consortio* 36.
2   See *Familiaris Consortio* 36.

father and mother.[3] Spouses are supposed to love one another before their children, and this should be something evident and palpable.[4] In a certain sense, the love for one's child is rooted in and caused by the love for one's spouse. The children instinctively understand this: so much so, that it is impossible for children to experience true love from their father or mother unless their father or mother love one another. You cannot love your child except through loving your spouse. The reason for this is that the children experience themselves as being equally from their father and mother. Any rejection of the mother by the father, or the father by the mother is therefore experienced by the children as a rejection of themselves. The children should see their parents as united, not divided: they came from their parents as from one flesh, so also they should see that their parents share one heart and mind. This right order of love within a family provides a more perfect manifestation of the procession of the Holy Spirit from the Father and the Son as from a single principle.

Another foundational aspect of the education of children is that the parents should love the children with the same intensity of love, while also willing that each child strive for and realize the different goods for which each one is suited. For example, a father may encourage one of his sons to pursue a life devoted to study and learning, while he might encourage another to pursue a life devoted to active good works. In both cases, he loves his sons with equal intensity of love, while desiring unequal goods for them depending upon their unique gifts. This way of loving at once preserves the security of knowing that each is loved precisely on the basis of being a child of their father, while also recognizing the uniqueness and special beauty of each child.

It is also important that children understand that their parent's love for them is not an *effect* of their achievements; but to the

---

3   "The first communion is the one which is established and which develops between husband and wife." *Familiaris Consortio* 19.

4   In one very beautiful family I know, when the father comes home from work or a trip, and his children meet him at the door, he says to them first: "Where is your mother?" When he has found her and greeted her with affection, only then does he turn his full attention to the children.

contrary, their parent's love for them is the *cause* why they have expectations for their children to succeed and to achieve the goods of which they are capable. In this way the love of a parent reflects the love of God, since God's love for us is not an effect of our goodness, but rather the cause of our goodness. Children must be affirmed so that they understand and affectively feel that it is simply good for them to exist in the eyes of their parents. Yet affirmation does not stop by simply recognizing the goodness of their existence: it expresses itself through encouragement and discipline in order that the children be perfected through education.

Finally, the education of children should make absolutely clear that the greatest good shared by the parents is the children themselves. A new child is the greatest blessing God can bestow upon a family. I sometimes ask couples rhetorically: "What good would you give in exchange for your youngest child?" The answer is obvious, as is the immediate corollary: nothing could be better for a family than another child. Every new child is like a new incarnation of its parent's love, standing as an immortal and irrevocable sign of that love. Therefore, each child also signifies the eternal love which brought about the Incarnation of the Son of God, so that with each child there is also born the hope of salvation. St. Paul explicitly connects child-bearing with salvation when he says that a "woman will be saved through bearing children."[5]

In materially prosperous nations, the parents are often presented with the choice between another child and a nicer home, or nicer things for their children, or more prestigious school for their children, or something of this sort. In such cases, the parents should be reminded that they are educating their children for Heaven not Harvard. This supernatural perspective on the final goal of Christian education is essential. No gift could be a better gift for a child than a brother or sister. Of course, there may be good and serious reasons why spouses might want to space the births of their children. For example, the physical or emotional health of the mother or father, the lack of basic necessities for family life, etc., are good reasons.

5 1 Tim 2:15 (RSV).

But all things being equal, the fundamental disposition of a married couple should be that the greatest blessing for their family is their children. This disposition will produce generosity and overcome unreasonable fears about bringing new life into the world.

Begetting children is a privileged form of total self-giving, and so it especially reflects the Trinitarian communion in which all the persons are mutually self-giving. In a special way, loving and begetting children as the supreme gift between spouses reflects the procession of the Holy Spirit, whose proper name is "Gift."[6]

DATING AND ENGAGED COUPLES

Courtship is a necessary and beautiful stage in the development of the person who is seeking to fulfill a vocation to marriage. A child who witnesses the love of his father and mother beholds that spousal communion as if from the *outside*. Through courtship, the person begins to *enter into* a communion like that found between spouses. This entering into communion with a member of the opposite sex is both a time of discernment and personal growth in the capacity for self-giving in the manner proper to spouses. Therefore, the first principle of courtship (today more commonly called "dating") is that it is ordained towards discerning marriage. Dating is not a form of entertainment or self-gratification, nor is it a means of balancing loneliness with the desire for freedom and self-determination.[7]

Although dating is a beginning of entering into spousal communion, it is important that the couple clearly understand the boundaries between the communion proper to dating and the communion proper to marriage. Obviously sexual intercourse is proper only to the married state, since it is ordered to the generation of children.

6 Cf., *S. T.*, Ia, q.38, a.2.

7 In fact, a right understanding of courtship and marriage sees that freedom is not sacrificed, but rather enhanced by entering into a more profound communion with others. The young man who gives up his ability to go out whenever he pleases when he gets married also gains the ability to beget and raise children by that same act. So he exchanges a lesser freedom for a greater freedom. Freedom is the ability to act in a way that perfects one's nature, and raising a family perfects human nature more than being able to go where one pleases when one pleases.

Cohabitation and sexual intimacy before marriage, aside from being serious sins, have lasting negative effects into the marriage itself. First of all, the couple have already engaged in the acts proper to marriage so that often they are confused about what makes them truly married. They think that marriage means a promise to live with one another for the rest of their lives, or to love one another for the rest of their lives, or to raise children together. But none of these make someone married. Unmarried persons might do all of these and still not be married. In marriage, the spouses give to one another, by a solemn and life-long vow, the exclusive right over each other's bodies for acts apt to generate children. If the couple has already been sexually intimate before the marriage, they often fail to see that marriage and exclusive sexual intimacy go hand-in-hand. Besides this, the husband often has more difficulty in trusting that his wife is faithful to him, and the wife tends to suspect her husband of seeking self-gratification even when he asks for legitimate sexual intimacy after marriage. The overall effect is that the blessings of marital intercourse are diminished for couples who were sexually intimate before marriage. It is as if they had mortgaged their marital intimacy before the marriage ever took place, and their experience of sexual intimacy in the marriage is impoverished as a result.

Not only sexual intercourse, but also any kind of physical intimacy (intimate touching, passionate kissing, etc.) which, in itself, *inclines* the emotions toward sexual intercourse is also proper to married communion. Another form of excessive familiarity to be avoided is spending a long time together alone in a private residence, or spending time alone together late at night or early in the morning in a private place. Even if such excessive familiarity were not an occasion of sin, this kind of living on familiar terms is one of the blessings of married life. To share a life so as to live together in the same home is proper to the communion of family life. And when a dating couple appropriates this kind of familiarity to themselves before marriage, they no longer experience it as a blessing proper to marriage. Instead, it is "just what couples do." On the other hand, couples who reserve this kind of living on familiar terms to their marriage, experience this form of intimacy as one of the blessings of marriage. In this way, the marriage bond is strengthened for both.

Some exaggerated forms of piety teach that a dating couple should show no more interest or affection toward each other than a brother and a sister. But this is clearly contrary to the aim of dating. A brother and sister could never discern marriage, so their interaction must have an essentially different character than a couple who is discerning marriage. For example, an intimate conversation about how to raise children together would not be appropriate for a brother and sister, but would be a necessary conversation for couples discerning marriage. Outward signs of affection and some form of exclusivity in the relationship are appropriate, so long as they are not in themselves ordered to (or likely to produce) sexual desire.[8]

Since dating is ordained towards marriage, the discernment involved in dating should focus upon the compatibility of a man and woman for coming together to form a family. This presupposes not only that each person possesses the requisite knowledge and moral virtues to enter freely and permanently into a marriage, as well as raise and provide for children. It also means that these two persons complement one another in the goods which are proper to marriage and family life. For example, if two persons are significantly unequal say in education, or culture, or maturity, this can be a serious impediment to marriage, in which spouses are supposed to relate to one another as equals, not like a parent to a child.

---

8   Sometimes an innocent gesture of affection such as holding hands or a brief hug arouses sexual desire. Such things are not in themselves disordered signs of affection, but if sexual desire comes about, the person in whom the desire comes about should discretely discontinue the affection until the desire goes away. Nor does this mean that he or she must always avoid such licit signs of affection in the future, since such things often depend upon bodily dispositions which frequently change. Licit signs of affection are good and important signs of love, so one should not be scrupulous and omit such licit and wholesome signs of love out of fear that some evil not intrinsically connected to the affection might come about. However, if someone can determine that sexual desire is nearly always aroused by such a sign of affection, he should let the other know about this and find some other manner of showing affection.

This discernment process will be greatly assisted if both parties are open and docile to the advice of their parents or others who know and love them well. Strong emotions tend to predominate between a young man and woman, and this can greatly obscure their ability to accurately judge their compatibility for marriage. In fact, one of the first things that dating couples need to be reminded about is that they are not one another's happiness. God has made us for himself, and only he can make us happy. To expect perfect happiness from another person is doomed to fail from the beginning, and will ultimately lead to disappointment and possibly divorce.

In a healthy courtship, the love of the couple for each other is not in competition with their love for God, but serves in a certain sense as a springboard for a greater appreciation of God's goodness found in the other. The goodness of the other is seen as having its origin in God, so that each person spontaneously moves from a love and appreciation of their beloved to a greater love and appreciation for God's goodness found in their beloved. Perhaps the best sign that a relationship is suited for marriage is that the concrete practice of love for God in each person is enhanced by the relationship, not diminished by it. To the contrary, if dating or engagement results in a diminishment of the concrete practice of charity toward God, then this is a sign that the couple is not suited for marriage. For example, if a young man or woman is in the habit of attending daily Mass and after they begin dating, they no longer have time for Mass, this is a sign that they are not leading one another closer to Christ. Jesus implies this in the parable about the great banquet: "Another said, 'I have just married a woman, and therefore I cannot come.'"9

NEWLY MARRIED COUPLES

Newly married couples are in a special way a sign of God's love and fidelity. God holds up the devotion of the people Israel in their first love for the Lord as a kind of standard of fidelity: "I remember

---

9 Lk 14:20 (NAB).

the devotion of your youth, how you loved me as a bride, following me in the desert, in a land unsown."[10] Despite the challenges
often posed by the adjustments of married life as well as financial
uncertainty and other obstacles, newly married couples tend to show
unfailing trust in one another and support for one another. Much of
this can be attributed to the assistance of the natural and powerful
emotions which accompany newly-experienced physical intimacy.
And while these emotions are fleeting, nevertheless, while they
persist, they tend to facilitate the unity of the spouses in the early
years of their marriage. And so they should be gratefully accepted as
something good and as a gift from God. This experience of new and
intense love, even if largely emotional, ought to remind the spouses
of the newness and intensity of love they should always bear towards
Christ, who is the bridegroom of every soul. So the life of newly
married spouses sets a kind of standard for the whole of married
life: not as regards the powerful positive emotions which exist in a
new marriage (for these are fleeting and not under our control), but
rather as regards the way in which spouses ought to choose to act
towards one another throughout their entire marriage.

It is important to remember at this stage in marriage, that the love
which the spouses have for one another is not meant to close the
couple in on themselves, but it is rather ordered to diffusing goodness to others. Newly married love has a certain fecundity which
ought to bear both physical and spiritual fruit. Marital intimacy is,
in itself, ordered to the generation of new life, while the Christian
love between spouses is ordered to manifesting the love of Christ for
his Church to the faithful who come into contact with the couple.
The goods of children and the sacramental sign are both common
goods meant to flow out upon the Church. Furthermore, hospitality
should be a hallmark of a newly married couple.

Newly married couples should set in place as soon as possible a
routine of prayer, penance and charitable works. This routine will
have to be modified, of course, as children come; but at every stage
of marriage there should be an expectation that these fundamental

10   Jer 2:2 (NAB). Cf. Hos 2:16-17.

Christian activities be ever present within the family, according to the ability and circumstances of each spouse.

Finally, it is inevitable that the powerful, positive emotions present at the beginning of married life will decrease in intensity. When these emotions fade, it is important not to think that the marriage is failing. To the contrary, only in this way can true love be intensified and the marriage be strengthened. This transitional time in a marriage is also meant to be a sign of those transitional times of darkness in the soul's relationship with Christ. True love does not look to the advantages which benefit the self, but rather those which benefit the other. So long as there are strong and pleasant emotions within a marriage, there will always be some doubt about whether the spouses are loving one another for the sake of the pleasant emotions, or for the sake of the other spouse. Once those pleasant emotions are gone or greatly diminished, only then can each spouse know for certain that their love is pure and truly directed at the good of the other.

A similar transition happens in our relationship with Christ. Jesus speaks about this in a parable from the Gospel of St. Luke:

> And he said to them: "Which of you shall have a friend, and shall go to him at midnight, and shall say to him: 'Friend, lend me three loaves, for a friend of mine has arrived on a journey, and I have nothing to set before him.' And he shall answer from within: 'Do not bother me, for the door is now shut, and my children are with me in bed. I cannot arise and give you anything.' Yet if he shall continue knocking, I tell you, though he will not arise and give him anything because he is his friend, yet because of his importunity he will rise and give him whatever he needs."[11]

We can read this parable about perseverance in prayer in a spiritual sense. For the "friend" within the house is God, our Father,

---

11   Lk 11:5-8 (NAB).

to whom our prayers are addressed. Jesus says that "he will go to him at midnight." Midnight is the time when the sun is exactly on the opposite side of the earth, so it is the time when light is farthest away. So Jesus says this to signify that this prayer is being made in the darkest trials of faith, the darkest times in our lives. Such dark times also take place in marriage. This darkness may be caused by evils in our lives: tragedies, sickness or depression, a sense of being unloved by one's spouse. Or it might be a spiritual, purifying trial of faith in which God permits us to feel lost and without any reason for our faith. "And he shall answer from within: Do not bother me, the door is now shut." The door seems to be shut to us because the Christian life can seem impossible to live at times, and we fall short of following and conforming ourselves to Christ who is the only way to the Father. "I cannot rise and give you anything." These words indicate the feeling of certitude we have during these dark times in our lives that we are rejected by God. It is as if we hear God saying to us: stop praying! But this is not the will of God, since he has commanded us to pray without ceasing (cf., Lk 18:1). But in spite of all these trials, the Lord solemnly assures us: "I tell you, though he will not arise and give him anything because he is his friend, yet because of his importunity, he will arise and give him whatever he needs." When we come to pray we might think that God will answer our prayers only if we are his friend, only if we are in a state of grace or holy like the saints. But Jesus tells us that is not true. Jesus tells us that what is more important than charity in prayer is perseverance; for not all who have charity at some point will receive what they pray for, but all who persevere to the end shall receive it. If God's gifts are bestowed upon us on account of our goodness, then the gifts we receive will be limited by the amount of our goodness. But if God's gifts are bestowed upon us on account of his goodness, then there is no limit to the goods we shall receive from him in prayer. The perseverance of married couples through these difficult times is a sign and witness of the perseverance to which the soul is called in its relationship with the Lord. He who perseveres to the end in marriage and in prayer shall obtain what he seeks.

11

Healing Corruptions of Family Life

ABOVE I HAVE ATTEMPTED TO DESCRIBE THE
ideal Christian family and how such a family comes into existence.
Healthy families tend to beget healthy families. But the Enemy of our
race is not content to allow such goodness to multiply unchecked,
and so he sows weeds among the beautiful flowers of the Christian
family. Original sin ruptured the original communion within the
first human family. When confronted by God about his sin, Adam
at once blames God and his wife: "The woman whom you put here
with me, she gave me fruit from the tree, so I ate it."[1] So also today,
the wound of original sin, together with the temptations of the Devil,
often results in corruptions in family life and a rupture in communion between God and man, between spouses, and between parents
and children.

As we have already seen, these corruptions distort our knowledge,
love and esteem for supernatural realities. Consider some particular
instances how the modern corruptions of the family can lead to
corruptions in faith. The indissolubility of marriage is intended to
be a sign of God's eternal and unique love for his Church. Is it any
surprise then that religious pluralism and the denial that there is
one Church is widespread in a society in which divorce and remarriage are widespread? And in households where, by design, there
is no father or there is no mother, how will the children come to
understand God as Father or what it means for God to love us like a
mother? Or how shall the spiritual motherhood of the Church or the
Virgin Mary be valued in a society which teaches that mothers are

---

1   Gen 3:12 (NAB).

expendable, a non-essential part of a family, which can be replaced by a man? And when the natural relationship between husband and wife is denied, the purpose of a male-only priesthood is misunderstood or rendered meaningless. Pope Francis underlines the significance of a male priesthood when he wrote that it is "a sign of Christ the Spouse who gives himself in the Eucharist."[2] Examples could be multiplied but, suffice it to say, a lack of love and esteem for the goodness of the natural family entails a lack of love and esteem for the inner life of God and the things of heaven.

In the modern world, such corruptions have become so serious and commonplace that, in some areas, the corruptions greatly outnumber the healthy families. These corruptions are of two kinds: those which involve a denial of the very nature of the family, and those which do not deny the nature of the family, but in some way destroy the right relationships within a family. We will first consider those which involve a denial of the very nature of the family, since these corruptions are more serious.

CORRUPTIONS DENYING THE NATURE OF MARRIAGE

Marriage, as asserted above, is something natural which has been elevated by Christ to something supernatural as a sacrament. The natural aspect of marriage is not unrelated to the supernatural aspect. To the contrary, the natural aspects of marriage serve as the very basis for the significance of marriage as a sacrament. For example, the natural indissolubility of marriage is the basis for the sacramental significance of the permanent union between Christ and the Church, and the permanent union between the divine and human nature in Christ. Therefore, denying the natural aspects of marriage involves a denial of the supernatural aspects of sacramental marriage.

Marriage as something natural can be defined as a natural and lifelong union between one man and one woman, entered into by free consent, for the sake of the generation and education of children. Each element of this definition has a corollary in the supernatural order. Corresponding to "lifelong union" is the permanent union

---

2 *Evangelium Gaudii* 104.

between Christ and the Church and the permanent union between the divinity and humanity in Christ, as well as the eternal communion among the Persons of the Trinity. Corresponding to "one man and one woman" is the one Christ and his one Church, and one divine and one human nature. Corresponding to "entered into by free consent" is the freedom with which Christ established the Church and took her to himself, and the freedom of each member of the Church to be united to Christ. Hence, no one can be baptized or receive any sacrament against their will. Corresponding to "for the sake of the generation and education of children" is the truth that the union of Christ and the Church is ordained to the regeneration and salvation of souls.

The most serious corruption of family life is that which denies that marriage is for the sake of the generation of children. To deny the intrinsic purpose of something is to deny everything else about that thing. If someone were to say that a knife is not for cutting, then there would be no reason for the knife to be hard or sharp or equipped with a handle for grasping. Everything about a knife would cease to be, so that there would be nothing left that one should call a "knife." Similarly, denying that marriage is for the sake of the generation and education of children implicitly denies everything about marriage.[3] If marriage is not for the sake of the generation and education of children, there is no reason why marriage should be between a man and a woman, or between one man and one woman, or natural, or lifelong, or even entered into by free consent.[4] And

---

3 Even those who expressly deny that marriage is for the sake of generating children implicitly admit this, since all admit that marriage involves sexual activity with the other person. Not any kind of union can be called marriage, but only that which arises from sexual love. And sexual love in itself is ordered to generation since it always involves the reproductive organs.

4 As discussed in detail in chapter 1 above, some people object to the position that marriage is for the sake of the generation and education of children by pointing out that infertile couples are allowed to marry. However, this is to fail to distinguish between what something *is for*, and what something *can actually do*. An eye is for seeing even if it loses its ability to see. A knife is for cutting even if it becomes too dull to cut. In fact, the reason why infertility of a couple, or blindness of an eye, or dullness of a knife are all seen as defects is precisely because they impede the proper purposes of the things to which they belong. We are simultaneously aware that they are *for something* which they

when these natural aspects of marriage are denied, their supernatural significance is also denied: the sacramentality of marriage is lost. Marriage would no longer be a sacrament of the fecundity of the Hypostatic Union or of the union between Christ and the Church. Nor does a union without the complementarity of male and female reflect the distinction of the divine and human in which the former gives and the latter is receptive.

Besides attempts to redefine marriage as including persons of the same gender (which obviously denies that marriage is for the sake of the generation of children), other corruptions deny certain aspects of the nature of marriage. Both polygamy and polyandry involve a denial of the nature of marriage, since both deny that marriage is between one man and one woman. At the sacramental level, this leads to a denial of the unity of the Church, contrary to the Creed in which believers confess that the Church is "one, holy, catholic and apostolic." Polygamy and polyandry also involve a denial at the sacramental level of the communion of life between God and man,[5] since peace and communion cannot be maintained in a household where there are multiple spouses. The practice of divorce and remarriage involves a denial of the same essential aspects of marriage. Divorce and remarriage is simply serial polygamy or polyandry: having one wife or husband at a time. In some ways this is worse than the case where the person remains together with multiple spouses at the same time. At least the polygamist is trying to be present as a father to all his children, while the divorced and remarried man often just sends a paycheck to his children. Communion is altogether broken between the remarried person and his prior family. A culture which

---

are *unable to do*. Both facts can exist side by side. So allowing infertile couples to marry does not involve denial that marriage is for the sake of generating children. Nor should the inability of a man and woman to generate children be confused with the inability of persons of the same sex to generate children. In the former case, there is an impeded natural ability, in the latter there is no natural ability at all. An infertile dog cannot have puppies, and an orange tree cannot have puppies. But it is clear that the word "cannot" in these two instances is used with a different meaning.

5   "Communion is radically contradicted by polygamy." *Familiaris Consortio* 19.

permits divorce and remarriage also denies the dogma that there is only one Church, since the principal sacramental sign of the unity of the Church is destroyed by divorce and remarriage.

The position that marriage is created by the state also denies the nature of marriage. In such a view, marriage is essentially a legal contract having existence because of the will of the authority in the state. And since marriage is the foundational relationship within a family, all other relationships in the family are also ultimately subject to the authority of the state. It is not difficult to see the error in this position. Marriage and family existed long before any state existed. Marriage arises from the natural inclination of our species to come together and beget children, as well as the natural inclination to stay together to care for our own children.[6] Men and women naturally love their children and want to care for them. No psychologically healthy individual needs to be taught or forced by the state to desire procreation or to care for their children. Again, the fact that jealousy naturally arises when one man is desired by many women, or one woman is desired by many men, is a sign that monogamy is also natural to man. People are not jealous because they read a state-made law that says they should be! Since marriage flows from the principles of human nature, not from laws, it follows that marriage is instituted by the one who instituted human nature, namely, God. This is also a truth revealed in the opening chapters of Genesis and in the Gospels: "What God has joined together, no human being must separate."[7] This natural foundation of marriage and family is intended to be a sign of the natural processions of the Son and the Holy Spirit in the divinity.

Finally, any position that a couple can be forced to marry against their will (such as arranged marriages against the consent of the parties, or state coerced marriages), denies something essential to the nature of marriage. Marriage must be entered into freely, since it involves a lifelong commitment which takes up the whole of one's

6 "The institution of marriage is not an undue interference by society or authority, nor the extrinsic imposition of a form. Rather, it is an interior requirement..." *Familiaris Consortio* 11.
7 Mk 10:9; Mt 19:6 (NAB).

life. Marriage is a relationship which involves the totality of the person, and the truest and greatest part of a human person is that by which he is free. Moreover, only love and not fear can be the basis of the communion proper to spouses and family life. The communion in a family must be an image of the communion of the Trinity.

In all these corruptions, the source is ignorance or error about the true nature of marriage and its supernatural significance. Ignorance of the nature of marriage arises from corrupt customs, often propagated by those who have power over the instruments of social communication.[8] The faithful should be careful to limit their use of social communication to those instruments which do not propagate erroneous ideas about the nature of marriage and family. This is especially important for children who have no means of defending themselves from false ideas. The faithful should also equip themselves with sound arguments which expose the most common false assertions about the family, and which manifest the false principles upon which they are based. For example, one such false principle which is used to justify false conceptions of family is the assertion that human reason is unable to determine with certitude the purposes of natural things. The supernatural significance of marriage should be taught in catechesis from an early age and also in homilies so that the faithful can see clearly the connection between the truth about marriage and the other fundamental doctrines of the Catholic Faith.

---

8   Pope John Paul II warns against the corruptive influence of mass media three times in *Familiaris Consortio*: "Not infrequently ideas and solutions which are very appealing but which obscure in varying degrees the truth and dignity of the human person, are offered to the men and women of today, in their deep search for a response to the important daily problems that affect their married and family life. These views are often supported by the powerful and pervasive organization of the means of social communication, which subtly endanger freedom and the capacity for objective judgment." *Familiaris Consortio* 4; "Under pressures coming above all from the mass media, the faithful do not always remain immune from the obscuring of certain fundamental values," (FC 7). Finally, the document adds that parents have a "duty . . . to protect the young from the forms of aggression they are subjected to by the mass media and to ensure that the use of the media in the family is carefully regulated." (FC 76).

CORRUPTIONS WHICH DESTROY RIGHT
RELATIONSHIPS WITHIN A FAMILY

Besides the corruptions which entail a denial of the nature of marriage and family, there are other corruptions which impede or destroy the right relationships within a family. Although these corruptions are less serious, they can still harm a family in a very grave manner. In fact, the bad experience of family members due to these corruptions sometimes leads to a denial of the very nature of marriage and family. This is similar to the way in which habitual venial sin prepares the way for mortal sin.

Since the generative act is the act proper to spouses, corruptions concerning the generative act harm the relationship between husband and wife in the most serious way. These corruptions include: contraception, artificial means of conception, adultery, and other forms of infidelity such as pornography and masturbation. All of these corruptions involve a denial of the truth that a reproductive act must be done reasonably: that is, in a manner that is in itself ordered to procreation exclusively with one's spouse. Only in this way can a reproductive act be an apt sign of the communication of goods between the human and divine. The Word assumed only one human nature, and through that human nature brought forth children of God.[9] Christ took to himself only one Church, and in taking the Church to himself on the Cross he intended to bring forth spiritual offspring: "Who ever heard of such a thing, or saw the like? Can a country be brought forth in one day, or a nation be born in a single moment? Yet Zion is scarcely in labor when she gives birth to her children."[10]

The power of reproduction is the essential power of all living things. It touches us at the most fundamental level, so that any disorder in the use of the reproductive power has harmful consequences in the whole life of a living being. Furthermore, for human beings, reproduction transcends the purely physical order since by means of a generative act, a new human person with an immaterial and

---

9   Cf., Jn 1:12-13.
10   Isa 66:8 (NAB).

immortal soul comes into existence. Moreover, as we have indicated above, the generative act itself is intended by God to be a sign of supernatural realities. A generative act which is in itself ordered to the begetting of a new human life is meant to be a sign that the union of the divine and human natures in Christ as well as the union of Christ with the Church are meant to beget new children in faith: "But to those who did accept him he gave power to become children of God, to those who believe in his name."[11] Contraception denies this supernatural significance of the generative act.[12] The natural begetting of a child through the loving union of husband and wife is intended to be a sign that God creates each human soul immediately and with love. This reality is obscured in a society which accepts *in vitro* fertilization or other artificial means of procreation. The eternal and natural procession of the Son from the Father is signified by the natural begetting of a child, yet this significance is lost to a society which accepts cloning or other non-natural modes of reproduction. In such a world, God, if one believes in him at all, will simply be viewed as a technician, a maker who stands apart from and indifferent to his creation.

Another very serious corruption which harms the right relationships within families is physical and/or psychological abuse by one of the spouses or parents. This abuse is an expression of the desire to dominate another rather than an expression of love which seeks the good of the other. Hence, abuse is to be distinguished from legitimate discipline which is ordered toward the correction and good of the one being disciplined. Yet it is not enough that such discipline be motivated by love: it must also be carried out in a way that expresses love. For example, punishment must not communicate rejection, but rather a desire for amendment which makes reunion possible.

Abuse is so serious because it destroys communion within a family. Domination is not a sharing of life. To the contrary, it manifests that the one who dominates does not want to share a life, but rather

---

11   Jn 1:12 (NAB).
12   Is it merely a coincidence that in those places where contraception is widespread among Catholics, a missionary spirit is lacking?

to treat the other as a slave; and on the part of the one who suffers abuse, it places an obstacle to their ability to share their life with the other spouse or parent. In a family where abuse takes place, the communion within the Trinity and between the human and divine natures in Christ is not signified. The children and spouses are therefore impeded from understanding and loving the communion of the Trinity and Incarnation.

HEALING CORRUPTIONS IN THE FAMILY

The first thing that must be laid down and accepted if these corruptions are to be healed within a family is the indispensable need for conversion: "What is needed is a continuous, permanent conversion."[13] Unless the persons within a family are willing to admit their moral faults and to make a firm purpose of amendment, there will be no possibility of healing. Often it happens that some members of a family are willing to convert, but others are not. In such cases, full communion cannot be restored,[14] and the persons who are willing to convert and do penance should ask forgiveness of those they have offended and turn to the Lord as their source of comfort and communion. While it is painful to live in such circumstances, no one can be truly harmed by the moral fault of another. Only our own moral fault causes us true harm.

Spouses must also adopt an attitude of mercy over and above a demand for justice. From the time we are children, we learn that the family is a place where we find mercy rather than justice, where each member does their duty regardless of whether others are fulfilling their duties. Small children give little or nothing, but receive everything from their parents and siblings. There is no justice

13 *Familiaris Consortio* 9.

14 In particularly abusive relationships, it may be necessary for one spouse to separate from the other in order to acquire some kind of stability and at least imperfect communion for the remaining family members. Yet even in such cases, the spouse who has separated ought to encourage their children to love and desire the healing of the abusive spouse. The love of one spouse must not be destroyed by the moral defects of the other spouse. Rather, their love ought to express itself in doing what they can for the moral healing of their spouse.

                     Part III: Practical Applications to Families

here. Spouses too must remember that their vows were not conditional. Spouses do not promise to be faithful and to love *only if* the other is faithful and loves. Nor should spouses "keep score," that is, constantly keep track of the good they have done for their spouse and demand a like return. Nothing destroys a family like the demand for strict justice.

Sometimes it is asked whether one should forgive a family member if they refuse to ask forgiveness or even fail to acknowledge that they have sinned. We should always be ready to forgive, but forgiveness itself -- entering into communion once again with the offending person, is something that requires repentance on the part of the offender. In fact, typically it would not be good for the one who has sinned to be treated as if he had not sinned, since this would result in his failing to convert, which would be to his moral harm. St. Augustine teaches: "If you are ready to forgive, you have already forgiven. Hold yourself to this that you pray: pray for him that he may ask pardon from you, because you know that it is harmful to him if he does not ask, [so] pray for him that he does ask."[15] Sometimes, however, one can prudently judge that offering forgiveness in words or other signs to one who has not yet acknowledged his guilt is likely to move him to contrition and repentance. In such a case it is permitted to offer words and other signs of forgiveness even if they do not ask for forgiveness.

Another step that must be taken if there is to be healing in a family is that the family members must explicitly acknowledge that they cannot expect to find happiness in one another. Very often, spouses (and sometimes parents and children) think that they will find happiness in one another, and when that does not happen, they are bitterly disappointed and even begin to hate one another. But the truth is that only God can make us happy, and trying to get happiness from another human person is like trying to squeeze blood out of a turnip. It is not fair to demand happiness from your spouse or your children or your parents. They are incapable of giving it to you even if they tried their very best. The purpose of

---

15   Sermon 211.

family relationships is not to lead us to find our happiness in one another, but in God.

Very often I have seen cases where two spouses are bitterly upset with one another, and each complains that the reason for their bitterness is that the other does not love them enough. The most important thing for each of them is being loved by the other, and yet, they hate each other: a great irony. For whatever reason neither is capable of showing love to the other in a way that the other can experience. But the root problem is that they want to be loved more than to love, and this is the secret of misery. For healing to take place, each family member must commit themselves to loving without expecting love in return. Being loved does not make someone a good person, but loving others does make someone a good person. But in order to have the strength to begin to love without expecting love in return, we need to experience being loved by God. When his love pours into our hearts, then we will have a sufficient supply to give to others. "We love because he first loved us."[16]

Another step that should be taken to heal corruptions in family life is to draw close to a flourishing Christian family. Just as damaged cells in a body are healed through contact with healthy cells, so also are damaged families healed by contact with healthy families. This is perhaps the most effective way to overcome corruptions in family communion. For example, in a family where no father is present, the children who are missing their father can see the healthy interaction of a father with his children in a flourishing family. This at once enkindles in the children a desire for a healthy relationship with a father, and convinces them of the goodness of having such a healthy relationship. Often, in such cases, the father or mother in a healthy family takes on the role of spiritual father or mother for those who lack healthy relationships with their parents. Many a soul has learned how to live a fruitful and faith-filled family life through friendship with a flourishing Christian family.

Another effective way of healing a defective family is by contact with a healthy religious community. Such an affiliation can

16   1 Jn 4:19 (NAB).

greatly supplement the assistance which comes from friendship with a healthy family, since it strengthens the focus on living a truly supernatural life. Spending time together with a religious community at their public hours of prayer, attending conferences by knowledgeable priests and religious, and introducing similar practices into one's home (such as praying the Divine Office together) are great sources of strength and spiritual healing.[17] In some cases, it can be beneficial to seek spiritual guidance on a regular basis from a prudent priest or religious. All of these practices re-orient the soul toward the things of heaven, and allow one to see their trials and troubles from the trusting perspective of God's providence. In short we can say that communion begets communion. Those who come into contact with the goodness and beauty of true communion, are drawn into that goodness and enabled to share in it themselves.

Finally, in order to heal corruptions within the family, it is essential to practice devotion to the Holy Family, as well as to each of its individual members. Devotion to the Sacred Heart in all of its approved forms will be a great consolation and assurance of divine love for those who suffer from rejection within their own families. Especially to be recommended is devotion to the Immaculate Heart of Mary through the common recitation of the Rosary. May the Immaculate Heart of Mary, which was so loved by Jesus and St. Joseph, be a source of unity and healing in all families who are in need of a mother's tender care and love. Amen.

---

17   Cf., *Familiaris Consortio* 61 and 74.

Additional Objections and Replies to the Definition of Marriage

Objection 14: You can't expect people to go without sex and companionship of a spouse. So it's wrong to prevent people from remarrying.

Answer: If human beings were merely animals without reason, then this argument would follow. For animals the greatest good they can attain is the propagation of their species, and so reproduction is their greatest good. But this is not true for human beings. Human beings have reason and therefore their greatest good is not sexual pleasure or reproduction, but a life lived according to what is best in them: the mind. Consequently, the greatest evil is not being deprived of sex. Rather, the greatest evil is being deprived of virtue.

The truth is that we do expect people to go without sex, even for an indefinite period of time, because human happiness is not found in the reproductive act or sexual pleasure. If for some reason a spouse becomes incapable of performing the reproductive act (e.g., sickness, or some accident, etc.) we expect the other spouse to remain faithful. If a husband is held as a prisoner of war for years we expect their wife to remain faithful. We do not say that she can't be expected to live without sex. So too, if one spouse abandons the other, this does not mean that the abandoned spouse is free to be unfaithful. Marriage vows are not made conditionally: "If you remain faithful, then I will." Rather, they are made unilaterally and unconditionally by both spouses: "I promise to remain faithful all the days of my life." This shows that the other spouse is loved for their own sake. It is true, however, that a spouse who, for no truly compelling reason, refuses sexual relations does something seriously wrong and is in part responsible if their spouse, failing from weakness, becomes unfaithful.

Objection 15: But if the whole reason why marriage should be lifelong is because of the children, it seems that at least couples without children are not obliged to stay together.

Answer: The reason why marriage should be lifelong is not because children *actually* come to be from the marriage, but because it is for the *purpose of* begetting and raising children. And even if no children come, it is perfective of human nature to be married and to remain married. True, it would be better to have the final perfection of actually begetting and raising children, but this does not diminish the value of the intermediate perfection of a life lived in married communion. Just because something is not the best does not mean that it is not good. Every perfection leading up to the perfection of begetting and raising children is itself good and perfective of human nature. For example, even if someone was not able to beget children, it would still be good for them to have otherwise healthy reproductive organs. Similarly, the virtue of generosity is for the sake of helping the poor, yet even if there are no poor to be helped, it is good to have the inclination to help the poor and it remains essential if someone is to be truly called "generous." Nature also imitates this. Blossoms on fruit trees are for the sake of pollination and bearing fruit. But even if the tree cannot bear fruit because there is no pollination, it is good for the trees to blossom.

Objection 16: But it seems that if someone fertile is married to someone who is infertile, the fertile spouse should be free to remarry. For it would be better for the species if the fertile spouse could beget children.

Answer: This objection implicitly holds that all marriage vows could be conditional: "If you are fertile, then I will remain faithful to you, but if not I can remarry." A vow which is conditional is unable by its very nature to be the basis for a stable union. Moreover, it would be a sign that the spouse is not loved for his own sake, but only for the sake of children. So there could be no true communion based upon such a vow. So while permitting people to remarry in case of infertility might contribute to the good of the species in some small number of instances by providing more children, the common good of the species would be harmed much more due to the instability resulting from the conditional vow of fidelity. For the instability in families would result in less healthy marriages and families, and fewer persons capable of raising children well. Moreover, since it happens naturally in nearly every marriage that the woman becomes infertile well before the man ceases to be able to generate children, it would follow from this reasoning that men should divorce their wives after they reach middle age in nearly all marriages! Such an attitude would be clearly harmful to the common good of all families.

Besides these reasons, the fact that there are a minority of infertile young couples may actually benefit the common good, since young couples who cannot have children are more inclined to adopt the children whose parents cannot care for them.

Objection 17: But since marriage is for the sake of children, it seems that spouses should love each other for the sake of the children. And if there are no children, then there seems to be no reason for them to love one another and stay together.

Answer: It does not follow that because marriage is for the sake of children that the spouses should love one another for the sake of children. In fact, the purpose of the marriage is best served when the spouses love one another for their own sake (i.e., desire and act for the true good and happiness of their spouse). This is because it is better for the children if the marriage is as stable as it can be, and a marriage where the spouses love one another for their own sake is much more stable than a marriage where the spouses love one another for the sake of something else (even if that something else is the children). Most children are aware of this. For example, children would rather see their parents angry at them than angry at one another. This does not mean that parents should not love their children, but it does mean that spouses should not love their children more than one another.

Objection 18: There are no such things as stable natures. Evolution proves that natures are always changing. So marriage and family must change as well.

Answer: This objection takes us a bit too far afield from the definition of the family to take up here in a satisfactory manner. However, this objection is covered more fully in the questions for chapter 2 on following reason and nature. At this juncture, I will simply point out two things. First of all, evolution does not posit that the nature of this or that individual is not stable. Evolution is supposed to work through the mechanism of reproduction, and so it does not refer to a change of nature in an individual, but rather it refers to the offspring having a different nature from the parent. Moreover, if there is one thing that evolution cannot, in principle, destroy, it is the inclination to reproduce successfully. Secondly, hunger and the desire to breathe are natural desires, and no one thinks that human beings will move past these desires. But the desire to reproduce is even more fundamental than hunger or the desire to breathe, since hunger and the desire to breathe belongs only to certain animals, but reproduction is common to all living things, not just human beings or animals. So that must mean that our natures are stable after all, especially in regard to matters of reproduction.

Objection 19: Homosexual inclinations are natural, and so same-sex unions are just as natural as opposite-sex unions. And this is not just true for humans: for example, many animal species exhibit homosexual behavior. Therefore, they should be called marriages in the same sense.

Answer: Even if one were to admit the premise that homosexual inclinations are natural, still it would not follow that homosexual unions should be called marriages in the same sense as marriage defined above. Marriage is for the sake of generating children. Homosexual unions are not. A different purpose means a different thing being defined.

But it can be clearly shown that homosexual inclinations are not natural. The first sense of natural inclination is a *tendency to perform actions which are necessary for the continued existence of the nature.*

If the inclination to reproduce between men and women were taken away, the entire human race would cease to exist. But if homosexual inclinations were taken away, the species would continue to exist (and probably increase more rapidly). This is a plain difference that clearly shows the radical difference between these inclinations.

Nor are homosexual actions necessary for the *well-being* of human nature. While friendship is necessary for the well-being of human nature, the use of reproductive organs in a way that frustrates their purpose is not necessary for the well-being of human nature. The only effect essentially linked to frustrating the purpose of reproductive organs is a failure to produce new members of our species, which, in itself, is clearly contrary to the good of human nature.

As we have shown above, "natural inclinations" are not the same as "conscious desires or inclinations we cannot choose not to have." A natural inclination arises from the kind of being something is and objectively perfects that nature. For example, it belongs to the nature of fish to breathe underwater, and breathing underwater is good for fish. It belongs to the nature of orange trees to produce oranges, and producing oranges is good for orange trees.

Someone might say that a natural desire is one we are born with, and people are born with homosexual desires. But the truth is that no one is born with sexual desires. Newborn babies do not experience sexual desires, nor does anyone remember having such desires when they were born! They normally come to have sexual desires during puberty when the reproductive organs develop. So when someone asserts that someone is born with homosexual inclinations (and hence they are natural), they usually mean that the people who have them did not choose to have them. As soon as they were aware of sexual desires (e.g., at the onset of puberty), they noticed that these desires were directed toward persons of the same sex. But this does not prove that these desires are natural even in the restricted sense of "inclinations one is born with." One simple explanation is that these desires could be caused by trauma prior to puberty. So the only conclusion one could reasonably draw from the fact that people have these desires is that they are not always the effect of our own choices.

In addition to this, not every inclination we are born with is good. Some people are born with genetic dispositions for alcoholism, cancer, mental illness, etc. All men are born with original sin, which includes the inclination to use our reproductive power unreasonably. Most men, for example, find themselves tempted to fornication or adultery at some point in their lives. So even if a person were born with the inclination for homosexual desires, this would not make it good or natural in the sense of something perfective of human nature.

Finally, even if *all* the members of another species exhibited homosexual behavior (which no species does, otherwise the species would die out) this has no bearing on *human* behavior. After all, some species kill their mates. Should we justify the occasional case where a man or woman kills their spouse because of this behavior in another species? Some species will kill their young: should we justify this in human beings? In fact, many biologists disagree with the claim that the behavior of some animals is homosexual, and most of the evidence put forward for that position is weak (for example, it is mostly taken from animals in captivity). But even if such behavior were established to exist among certain members of another species in their natural habitat, this would not mean that homosexual actions are natural and good for human beings. Nor would it mean that it is even good for that species. For in every species of animal it is typical to find disordered actions among certain members. Some whales beach themselves; some animals eat food that is unhealthy or even poisonous for them. So if an animal uses a reproductive organ in a way that makes reproduction impossible, this is similar to an animal using its power of eating to eat something that can't be nutritious: it's still not good for the animal or its species.

Objection 20: Nothing could be more natural than the desire to have sex. But this desire exists whether or not someone is married. Therefore, sex with someone you are not married to is natural, and not exclusive to marriage.

Answer: This is not an objection to the definition of marriage, it is simply a tangential question that arises from my assertion that the desire to reproduce is natural. That being said, when an inclination is natural, this refers to the specific nature of a thing, not merely the common aspects of that nature. For example, just because human beings have natural desires to eat, drink and expel waste, does not mean that we can do these things in the same way that other animals do. Man is not just an animal; man is an animal with reason. And so we have to eat in a reasonable way, and drink in a reasonable way, and go to the bathroom in a reasonable way, not on the neighbor's lawn like other animals. Similarly, it is natural for human beings to reproduce in a reasonable way, not like other animals. But our reason tells us that it would not be good for children to come into the world without parents in a stable, loving union. Therefore, it is not natural for human beings to have sex without being married.

Objection 21: The only reason to get married is as a social convention to make sure someone is responsible for the children that come from sex. But there are ways to have sex now which ensure that children will not come about (namely, contraception). And certainly, elderly couples do not have to worry about children. Therefore, marriage is no longer necessary, and it is perfectly reasonable to have sex so long as someone uses contraception.

Answer: First of all, the reason for marriage is not merely so that the children will not become a burden on society. Marriage is not only good for the society, but it is also good for the persons who marry. Ask any couple as they are about to marry whether they are merely marrying for the good of society, and that should manifest the falseness of the statement that marriage is only for the sake of relieving the society of the burden of caring for children. It is good for a man and woman to live in communion. It is good for a man and woman to beget and raise their children. These activities are not merely to help society. Moreover, even if children do not actually come of marriage, marriage fulfills the natural inclinations of the spouses. It is perfective of the persons (the husband and wife) themselves. As noted above, what a thing is able to do, and what it is supposed to do are two different realities. And even if something cannot do what it is supposed to do (e.g., an orange tree cannot bear oranges), as much as possible it still should be treated in a way that supports the actions it is supposed to do (e.g., an infertile orange tree should be planted in good soil and watered regularly).

Secondly, using contraception (and *a fortiori* abortion) is against reason and contrary to human nature. Reason sees that the purpose of our reproductive organs is (not surprisingly) to reproduce. And to use them in a way which makes reproduction impossible is wrong, much as eating glass, or some other indigestible material, would be disordered.

Objection 22: Some people desire to be married to many persons at the same time. And each person should be able to follow their individual desires. We should live and let live, rather than forcing others to conform to what the majority happen to desire.

Answer: Once again, this objection stems from a confusion between emotional or conscious desire and natural desire (see the response to objection 10 in chapter 1). As we have seen, human nature is perfected by marriage to only one person, not many. A sign of this is the natural jealousies that arise between men and women when one man is the desire of many women, or when one woman is the desire of many men. Fathers rightly desire to know who their own children are, and there is no natural way for this to happen, unless the mother is faithful to him alone, and they both know this. It is natural for a man and woman to love each other before conceiving a child, so that it is natural for them to have a kind of friendship and equality — and hence the man, too, should have only one wife, otherwise that equality would be lacking. Finally, raising a human child requires living with the child for many years, and making great sacrifices of time & energy. If we have more than one spouse, and hence more than one set of children, our attention is divided, and the bonds of friendship weakened — which is not good for spouses or children (It is hard enough even when we just try to please one spouse and one set of children). All of these facts are objective realities about human nature, not descriptions of how people subjectively feel. Therefore, we are by nature inclined to have just one spouse.

As far as letting persons follow their own desires, no one thinks this is universally true. Should a drug addict be free to overdose on heroin? Should a father be free to follow his desire to have sex with his own child? Should a child molester be free to follow his own desires? Should a serial killer be free to follow his desire to murder? Examples could be multiplied, but suffice it to say everyone admits that some desires cannot be followed: we can't live and let live in every case. Some desires harm others and ourselves. The desire to have multiple spouses is a desire of this kind: it harms any children that might come of the union, and it harms the spouses themselves, since it does not bring them to virtue or happiness. Finally, it harms the society as a whole since it teaches others in the society that there is no significant benefit to monogamy, which is false. I will have more to say on this point in chapter 2 on the right use of freedom.

Objection 23: Free consent is not necessary to make a marriage. Most of marriages in history were arranged marriages.

Answer: Even in an arranged marriage free consent is required for marriage. A person is always free to reject the spouse proposed in an arranged marriage, and any attempt to force them to marry against their will would result in an invalid marriage. It is contrary to reason to expect two persons to enter into a lifelong commitment such as marriage without their free consent. This teaching was recognized throughout history by those who considered the nature of marriage, even in cultures where marriages were arranged (for example, St. John Chrysostom and St. Thomas Aquinas both clearly taught that marriage requires free consent even though marriage was arranged in their cultures). If at some places and times in history the right of the spouses to make free consent was denied, this only indicates that marriage was wrongly understood in those cases.

Objection 24: Loving one another is more important than being related by blood. So my real family are those whom I love and those who love me.

Answer: Implied in this objection is the assumption that someone does not love their family and is not loved by their family. It seems that the objection would never be raised by someone who has a healthy family life where the love which ought to exist is present.

And so this is not an objection against marriage and family as such, but an objection against unhealthy, dysfunctional marriages and families. So the real problem is not marriage or family as they have been defined above. Instead, the real problem is the lack of love in the hearts of the family members. They certainly do not lack love for one another *because* they are family members, but rather *in spite* of the fact that they are family members.

Friendship is an extremely important part of human life, and in some respects can even be more important than family relationships based upon blood ties. Yet this does not mean that friendships should be treated the same as family relationships, nor does it justify treating family members merely as friends. This is especially true in the case of relationships within one's immediate family: husband, wife, and children.

Because of the natural inclinations of spouses to reproduce, and to remain together to raise their own children; and because of the natural inclination of children to honor, show gratitude, and obey their parents as the source of their existence, relationships within the immediate family are unique and cannot be replaced merely by the love of friendship. As a result of these natural inclinations, certain rights and duties belong to family members which could never belong to mere friends. Spouses have certain rights and duties as regards fidelity to one another which friends do not have. Cheating on your spouse is adultery. Cheating on your friend is not. Parents have the right and duty to raise and educate their own children, and if they fail in their duty they should be compelled by society to fulfill them to the extent that this is possible. On the other hand, no friend should be compelled to do this. Similarly, children have a duty to honor and obey their own parents, and if they fail in this they should be corrected. Children have received the gift of life from their parents, a gift they could never repay. This is an objective relationship they have towards their parents that is unlike any other human relationship, and mere friendship could never make such a claim on someone. In brief, friendship is not held to the same standard as immediate family relationships because it is not based upon the same natural inclinations.

ABOUT THE AUTHOR

Born in Los Angeles in 1969, Fr. Sebastian Walshe entered the Abbey of St. Michael in the Diocese of Orange, California in 1998, and was ordained a priest in 2005. He is a professor of Philosophy for the seminary program. After completing his studies at Thomas Aquinas College in California, he continued studies at The Catholic University of America in Washington D.C., receiving a license in Philosophy. Later, he attended the Pontifical University of St. Thomas at Rome (the Angelicum) where he received a Masters in Sacred Theology and a Doctorate in Philosophy. His thesis was entitled: *The Primacy of the Common Good as the Root of Personal Dignity in the Doctrine of St. Thomas Aquinas.* From 2003–2005, Fr. Sebastian was also a visiting professor in the Philosophy Department at the Angelicum. Fr. Sebastian is also a regular guest on the Catholic Answers Live radio show. He is the author of the forthcoming titles: *Secrets from Heaven: Hidden Treasures of Faith in the Parables and Conversations of Jesus* and *Keeping Your Kids Catholic* published by Catholic Answers.

RECENT TITLES
AROUCA PRESS

Integrity, Volume 1 (October–December 1946)
Edited by Carol Robinson & Ed Willock

Integrity, Volume 2 (January–June 1947)
Edited by Carol Robinson & Ed Willock

The Eightfold Kingdom Within:
Essays on the Beatitudes and the Gifts of the Holy Ghost
Carol Jackson Robinson

Liberalism: A Critique of Its Basic
Principles and Various Forms
Louis Cardinal Billot, S.J.
(Newly translated by Thomas Storck)

Sundays & Festivals with the Fathers of the Church:
Homilies on the Gospels of the Ecclesiastical Year
Rev. D.G. Hubert

The Pearl of Great Price:
Pius VI & the Sack of Rome
Christian Browne

CPSIA information can be obtained
at www.ICGtesting.com
Printed in the USA
FSHW010949270720
72497FS